Great Books
for Independent Reading
50 Synopses, Quizzes, Tests, & Answer Keys

VOLUME 3

Bonnie A. Helms

J. Weston Walch, Publisher
Portland, Maine

Notes of Appreciation

To Deborah Locke for her help in suggesting titles and obtaining library materials.

To Margaret Hughes and Susan Julavits for assistance
in field-testing sample pages with their classes.

To Maurice and Mary Jane Stone for their support, love and encouragement
while this book was in process.

Users' Guide to
Walch Reproducible Books

As part of our general effort to provide educational materials which are as practical and economical as possible, we have designated this publication a "reproducible book." The designation means that purchase of the book includes purchase of the right to limited reproduction of all pages on which this symbol appears:

Here is the basic Walch policy: We grant to individual purchasers of this book the right to make sufficient copies of reproducible pages for use by all students of a single teacher. This permission is limited to a single teacher, and does not apply to entire schools or school systems, so institutions purchasing the book should pass the permission on to a single teacher. Copying of the book or its parts for resale is prohibited.

Any questions regarding this policy or requests to purchase further reproduction rights should be addressed to:

Permissions Editor
J. Weston Walch, Publisher
P.O. Box 658
Portland, ME 04104-0658

Reproduction is permitted for library and resource center use, provided that one copy of this publication is purchased for each 100 students expected to use it in a given academic year. Reproducing class lots of library or resource center copies of this publication for use in traditional classrooms is not permitted. When such copies are desired, purchase of a separate publication for each using teacher is required.

1   2   3   4   5   6   7   8   9   10

0-8251-2053-5

Originally published as *150 Great Books*
Copyright © 1986, 1991
J. Weston Walch, Publisher
P.O. Box 658 • Portland, Maine 04104-0658

Printed in the United States of America

Contents

Letter indication before each title refers to the reading level: Easy, Medium, or Challenging. Answer keys for the tests in each section appear at the end of that section.

To the Teacher v

Glossary of Literary Terms vii

UNIT 1—The Inner Journey

SYNOPSES   3–8

QUIZZES AND TESTS

M	*When the Legends Die*	Hal Borland	9
M	*Jane Eyre*	Charlotte Brontë	11
M	*Great Expectations*	Charles Dickens	13
E	*The Summer of My German Soldier*	Bette Greene	15
E	*Tex*	S.E. Hinton	17
C	*The Metamorphosis*	Franz Kafka	19
E	*A Separate Peace*	John Knowles	21
M	*Christy*	Catherine Marshall	23
M	*The Heart is a Lonely Hunter*	Carson McCullers	25
M	*The Member of the Wedding*	Carson McCullers	27
M	*The Chosen*	Chaim Potok	29
M	*The Catcher in the Rye*	J.D. Salinger	31
E	*Shane*	Jack Schaefer	33
E	*The Odd Couple*	Neil Simon	35
C	*Rabbit, Run*	John Updike	37
M	*Macho*	Edmund Villasenor	39

ANSWER KEYS   41

UNIT 2—Steps Back in Time

SYNOPSES   51-56

QUIZZES AND TESTS

M	*Elizabeth the Queen*	Maxwell Anderson	57
M	*Becket*	Jean Anouilh	59
C	*A Tale of Two Cities*	Charles Dickens	61
E	*April Morning*	Howard Fast	63
M	*Cimarron*	Edna Ferber	65
M	*The Great Gatsby*	F. Scott Fitzgerald	67
E	*Johnny Tremain*	Esther Forbes	69
M	*The Lion in Winter*	James Goldman	71
C	*The House of the Seven Gables*	Nathaniel Hawthorne	73
C	*The Scarlet Letter*	Nathaniel Hawthorne	75
M	*The Country of the Pointed Firs*	Sarah Orne Jewett	77
C	*Doctor Zhivago*	Boris Pasternak	79
C	*The Winthrop Woman*	Anya Seton	81
C	*Exodus*	Leon Uris	83
E	*The Friendly Persuasion*	Jessamyn West	85
M	*The Caine Mutiny Court-Martial*	Herman Wouk	87

ANSWER KEYS   89

UNIT 3—Questions of Conscience

SYNOPSES   99–104

QUIZZES AND TESTS

E	*To Sir With Love*	E.R. Braithwaite	105
M	*The Good Earth*	Pearl Buck	107
E	*The Chocolate War*	Robert Cormier	109
M	*I Am the Cheese*	Robert Cormier	111
E	*The Autobiography of Miss Jane Pittman*	Ernest J. Gaines	113
M	*Black Like Me*	John Howard Griffin	115
M	*A Raisin in the Sun*	Lorraine Hansbury	117
M	*The Little Foxes*	Lillian Hellman	119
E	*Inherit the Wind*	Jerome Lawrence and Robert E. Lee	121
M	*To Kill a Mockingbird*	Harper Lee	123
M	*Main Street*	Sinclair Lewis	125
M	*The Crucible*	Arthur Miller	127
E	*Animal Farm*	George Orwell	129
M	*Cry, the Beloved Country*	Alan Paton	131
M	*Twelve Angry Men*	Reginald Rose	133
M	*A Majority of One*	Leonard Spigelgass	135
E	*The Hiding Place*	Corrie Ten Boom	137
C	*Native Son*	Richard Wright	139

ANSWER KEYS   141

To the Teacher

Reading good literature should open wide the windows of the world. A body of materials which will link the student in grades seven through twelve with the general experience of humankind is provided in *Great Books for Independent Reading*. Contact with the plots, themes, and imagery of various authors will begin to launch the mind of the student into the currents of human motivation for people in all times and places. The young reader will become aware that the same great questions have provided themes for writers of all historical ages, as the soul of humankind has always reached out for answers. The meaning of life, the inevitability of death, the quest for faith, the spirit of adventure, and the process of maturation into adulthood were of concern to the ancient Egyptian as they are to the citizen of the space age. A book that is worth reading is a book which considers one or more of these great human universals. While reading, the student should find in the novel, biography, or drama a piece of his or her own experience, a mirror for the mind. In his essay "A Platform and a Passion or Two," the American dramatist Thornton Wilder said that reading literature assumes meaningful human dimensions only when the reader can say, "This is the way things are. I have always known it without being fully aware that I knew it. Now in the presence of this play or novel or poem or picture or piece of music, I know that I know it." (*Adventures in American Literature*, Harcourt, Brace, Jovanovich, p. 744.)

Each test in this volume contains three types of questions: (1) A set of objective questions will measure the student's understanding of the reading content. Has the reader grasped the basics of plot, characterization, and setting which the author has presented? (2) Five short-answer questions require more inferential responses. What are the larger ideas that the author wishes the reader to grasp? Answering these questions will also help to develop the student's writing skills, as the directions require the responses to be written in complete sentences. (3) The challenge essay requires a more mature level of thinking. The reader is asked to relate the material in a specific book to wider areas of thought. How is this book related to other books on the same subject? The first two sets of questions are basically factual. The challenge essay asks the student to express observations on the work that has been read, to support those observations with information gained from reading, and to link those observations with wider human experience. Through the use of these challenge questions, the student may use the readings as raw material for learning the basics of expository writing forms.

If an entire class has read a particular title, the test in this collection may well be used for a closed-book evaluation. If the teacher does choose to use a particular test with the entire class, not all questions may be suitable for all students or groups of students. For example, in a heterogeneous classroom, the slower students might answer only the twenty objective questions. The more advanced students could exercise inferential reading skills by answering the short-answer and the essays. In an honors group or a writing class, the students might write only the challenge essay. The majority of these tests are designed to serve as open-book evaluations and to stimulate the student's independent reading program. Tests used in this manner may serve as alternatives to the more traditional book reports.

To guide the student in selecting books within the appropriate interest and ability range, the titles have been graded in the table of contents with three different designations: (E) indicates easy reading for students who may really be reluctant to read anything at all; (M) indicates medium or average-level titles which will present no problem for the student who is reading on grade level; (C) indicates longer or more challenging titles. These books provide the real challenge for the mature reader. Even though the reading may take more time and the student may consequently complete fewer titles, these (C) titles will be well worth the capable student's effort.

Each unit section of tests is followed by answer keys for the titles that appear in that section. Brief suggested answers are provided for the short-answer questions and the challenge essays. Teachers should allow the students some latitude in their short-answer and essay responses, since several possible answers may be equally correct. If the teacher questions a student's response, the teacher may require the student to prove his or her statement by reference to the book.

The most obvious uses for **Great Books for Independent Reading** will be in the English or Language Arts classroom. A copy would also be a valuable reference tool in the school library. The test materials could be used for evaluation of outside readings in social studies classes. Students can learn much by comparing the fictional treatment of historical subject matter with the presentation given in the history text. Information which may seem rather dull on the textbook page comes to life in the hands of a skilled craftsperson.

Since students and *parents* place such great importance on grades, methods of point evaluation must be developed for the use of these tests. These evaluation methods will vary widely. At the beginning of the year or of the semester, the teacher and the students may establish a point system for the evaluation of the outside reading. The student will receive points for the number of books read and for the number of test questions answered correctly. More difficult books should have greater point value. Challenge-essay answers should also have more point value. At the end of the grading period, the number of reading and writing points received would be included as a portion of the student's total grade average. During the quarter, the student may place each finished piece of work in a folder, which the teacher will evaluate every two or three weeks. Conference time should also be provided when the student can discuss the readings with the teacher. The importance of this independent reading program will be greatly emphasized if class time is set aside for reading, and if the teacher reads with the students. The teacher must remain flexible and must fit both the reading procedure and the evaluation techniques to the individual or to the class.

World literature is a giant smorgasbord. Many different writing styles and conflicting philosophies will appeal to many varied student interests. Not everyone will appreciate everything that is offered, but many special treats await each one that can be motivated to sample the feast. Teacher and student will gain a surface measure of the personal growth which comes from a varied independent reading program. As students learn of the universal truths which are the common denominators of life, they mature in understanding themselves and others. This mental growth moves readers from narrow thinking, bigotry, and prejudice toward the understanding that other people, though very different one from another, may be equally and wonderfully human.

May the titles included in this volume generate new excitement about reading for student and teacher alike.

Glossary of Literary Terms

Plot—a sequence of events; what happens in the story. In a standard work of fiction, the plot is divided into four sections: (1) Exposition—the introduction which establishes the setting and introduces the characters. (2) Rising action—a complication or problem develops. (3) Climax—the turning point in the action which determines the outcome. (4) Denouement—the events following the climax. Mysteries are unraveled and confusions are set straight.

Protagonist—the most important character in a work of fiction.

Antagonist—the major character or force opposing the main character.

Conflict—the tension or struggle between the protagonist and the antagonist. Without conflict, there would be no plot. Three basic kinds of conflict are most common in works of fiction: (1) Person against person; (2) Person against environment; (3) Person against self.

Foreshadowing—significant hints given by the author which help the reader predict the outcome of the action.

Flashback—a scene or scenes inserted to show events that happened before the action of the main plot.

Epiphany—the turning point, a moment of insight or awareness that changes a character's outlook significantly.

Characterization—methods by which an author makes his creations "live" for the reader. Common methods of character presentation include characterization by what the character thinks, says, and does; by what other characters say about him or her; by the author's physical description of looks, gestures, or habits.

Developing character—one who undergoes an important change or learns a significant lesson as a result of his or her experiences.

Static character—one whom experience has not changed.

Stock character—a type familiar to the reader. This character has occurred so often in fiction that the reader can predict behavior.

Flat character—one who has only one or two significant traits, who is presented as being either all good or all bad. Note: flat characters are often very important to the action.

Round character—one whom is "human." He or she is a complex mixture of strength and weakness, good and bad. In a well-developed novel, the protagonist is usually round.

Setting—the time and place of the action.

Mood—the emotion, feeling, atmosphere, or tone that a fictional work presents—for example, romance or terror. The mood in fiction is how the reader feels as he or she reads.

Theme—the central ideas or truths that a plot illustrates. Usually a novel will have one main theme and several lesser themes. The idea may be presented in two ways: (1) Explicit—the author states the theme or themes for the reader. (2) Implicit—the reader must infer the theme from the action and characterization.

Slant—the approach that an author takes toward human experience, the way that he or she sees life. Slant will play a large part in determining both characterization and theme.

Point of view—who is telling the story. There are two basic types: (1) First-person point of view—the story is told by one of the characters involved. (2) Third-person point of view—the story is told by the author or an outside narrator.

Viewpoint character—the character through whose eyes we see the action. An author must limit the viewpoint to what that character would experience or understand.

Irony—a situation with a twist in meaning. (1) Verbal irony—saying one thing, but meaning another. (2) Situational irony—one thing is expected to happen, but something else occurs. (3) Dramatic irony—the reader has information which the characters do not, and that knowledge significantly affects the outcome of the plot.

Historical novel—a plot presenting imaginary characters involved in actual historical events.

Sociological novel—a plot focusing on human relationships or social problems. These novels are frequently used as teaching vehicles to advocate social change.

Psychological novel—plot focuses on character development, usually of the protagonist. In these novels, the "inner landscape" of the character's mind frequently becomes the most important sphere of action.

Note: A multi-purpose novel may fit into more than one of these categories. For example, Margaret Mitchell's *Gone With the Wind* is a historical novel of the Civil War and also a psychological study of Scarlett O'Hara.

Biography—a life story written by an author other than the subject.

Autobiography—a life story written by the subject.

Unit 1
The Inner Journey

Synopses

When the Legends Die
by Hal Borland

Tom Black Bull is a young Indian who struggles for survival in a white man's world. After his parents are forced to flee from the reservation, Tom is brought up in the wilderness and is educated in the old ways of his people. After the death of Tom's parents, the boy becomes brother to a bear cub. Although Tom is brought back by Blue Elk, a traitor to his own people, the boy refuses to adapt to the humiliation of the reservation school. A skilled rider, Tom is found by Red Dillon, who uses the boy to win money on a "fixed" rodeo circuit. After Tom breaks Red's control on his life, the young Indian becomes "Killer Tom Black," who takes out his isolation and rage on the horses that he rides. After being seriously injured in a fall, Tom returns to Bald Mountain to recover his physical strength and to find his identity as a man and as an Indian. *When the Legends Die* considers whether an Indian must be assimilated into the white man's culture to survive. This novel is an important contribution to the literature of America's minority groups.

Jane Eyre
by Charlotte Brontë

Jane Eyre is a novel set in nineteenth-century England. The young heroine develops character as she struggles for love, survival, and human dignity. As a child, Jane suffers a great deal of abuse at the hands of her cruel aunt, Mrs. Reed. Sent to Lowood, a charity school for girls, Jane experiences further cruelty, but she also matures through the teaching of Miss Temple and the loving friendship of Helen Burns. Jane's desire for independence takes her to Thornfield Hall, where she is employed to teach Adele, the ward of Mr. Edward Rochester. Jane's relationship with Rochester ripens into love. Happiness, however, is shattered by the revelation of a dark secret from Rochester's past. Jane shows her strength in parting from Rochester. Her firm character also shines in her resistance to the strong personality of St. John Rivers. Jane's reunion with the man she really loves gives the novel a happy ending. *Jane Eyre* is a strong statement of the dignity of women and the rights of every individual.

Great Expectations
by Charles Dickens

Pip, a young English boy who lives in a nineteenth-century village, has been brought up by his cruel sister, Mrs. Joe Gargery. Pip's only friend is the kindly blacksmith Joe. After Pip meets the mysterious Miss Havisham and her beautiful ward, Estella, the lad becomes discontent and desires to be a gentleman. He is then told that he has "great expectations," which will be supplied by a mysterious benefactor. Dickens' masterpiece contains a host of marvelous characters: the fearful convict, the pompous Pumblechook, the lawyer Jaggers. Most of all, the novel traces the growth of Pip himself from boy to man. Filled with Gothic description and powerful social commentary, *Great Expectations* shows the reader the England of Dickens' time through Pip's eyes as the young hero learns to distinguish true values from false. A strong plot line is created by the mystery of Pip's unknown benefactor and his unrequited love for the beautiful Estella. This novel of passage is important to any student's reading experience.

The Summer of My German Soldier
by Bette Greene

Patty Bergen is a sensitive twelve-year-old Jewish girl who lives in Jenkins-ville, Arkansas in the 1940s. Wanting only to be loved, Patty is cruelly rejected by a self-centered mother and an abusive father. Her only solace is Ruth, the black housekeeper. When a group of German POWs is sent to Jenkinsville to pick cotton, Patty becomes friends with one special German, Anton Reiker. When Anton tries to escape, Patty hides and protects him. After Anton's departure, Patty must hold to the belief that she is a person of value, and not the criminal that the world proclaims her to be. Patty Bergen's needs are the needs of every person—to belong and to be loved. *The Summer of My German Soldier* is simply written, but the novel contains ideas to which students of all ability levels can relate.

Tex
by S.E. Hinton

Tex is another of this author's novels of teenagers surviving without adults. Tex lives with his older brother Mace. Their mother is dead, and their father is away on the rodeo circuit for many months at a time. Tex's great loves are horses and Jamie Collins, the girl next door. The novel contains exciting scenes as Tex is involved in confrontations with an escaped convict and a drug pusher. Tex matures as he battles with his feelings for Jamie, and is forced to cope with the truth about his own parentage. *Tex* presents to the teenage reader significant problems of making choices and accepting the consequences of those choices.

The Metamorphosis
by Franz Kafka

The Metamorphosis is a dark, absurdist story in which Gregor Samsa, an aver-age little man, is inexplicably transformed into a giant beetle. Gregor, who has been the chief support of his family, seeks their help in his dilemma. Although he is at first aided by his sister, Gregor is brutally rejected and attacked by his father. The novel's plot recounts Gregor's mental deterioration, total rejection, and death. *The Metamorphosis* is a significant work by one of modern literature's most tortured authors. Gregor's need is the need of all men—to find significance and security in personal relationships. Yet Gregor feels guilty and rejected for reasons the reader never understands. This puzzling story will provide a chal-lenge for the mature reader.

A Separate Peace
by John Knowles

Phineas and Gene are students at Devon Preparatory School in the early years of World War II. The story is told as a flashback as Gene returns to the campus years later. Phineas is an athlete whose outrageous behavior and charismatic personality quickly make him a school leader. Gene is the scholar who follows Phineas admiringly, yet is angered by Phineas' disruption of the academic routine. When a freak accident cripples Phineas, Gene tries to atone for his guilt in causing the mishap. The ruthless Brinker and the tragic Lenny play significant roles in Gene's growth as the war moves closer to Devon. Phineas' tragic death brings the story to its climax. Gene said that he could later face the war because he had met and conquered his enemy at Devon. *A Separate Peace* is a well-written account of one boy's march toward manhood.

Christy
by Catherine Marshall

Christy is a novel loosely based on the girlhood experiences of the author's mother. In 1912, idealistic young Christy Huddleston goes to teach school in the mountain community of Cutter Gap, Tennessee. Although horrified by the primitive living conditions and the barbaric superstitions, Christy also finds much love and beauty in the hearts of the mountain people. As Christy teaches, she encounters moonshiners and an epidemic of typhoid fever. The gentle beauty of Fairlight Spencer, the strong faith of Miss Alice Henderson, the mission teacher, and the determination of Dr. Neil MacNeill all help to transform Christy from a girl to a mature young woman. The author presents beautiful natural description and details of mountain life. *Christy* is a novel of faith and belief in the triumph of the human spirit.

The Heart is a Lonely Hunter
by Carson McCullers

The Heart is a Lonely Hunter is set in a small southern town in the 1930s. Mick Kelley, a young girl struggling to grow up, lives in the "outside room" of the real world and in the "inside room" of her imagination. Mick can communicate best with Mr. Singer, a watchmaker who boards with her family. Ironically, Singer himself is mute. Other characters who visit Singer with a need to communicate are Blount, a roving handyman, Biff Brannon, a widowed cafe owner, and Dr. Copeland, a black physician with a burning need to help his people. *The Heart is a Lonely Hunter* has a loosely unified plot. By opening up to Singer, each character finds the courage to grow. Sadly, Singer has no one. The gentle irony of the author's characterizations makes this novel well worth reading.

The Member of the Wedding
by Carson McCullers

This play, set in a small southern town in the 1930s, explores the need for belonging. Frankie Addams is a lonely girl with a gift for exaggerated fantasy. Her only companions are her cousin, John Henry, and Berenice, the black cook. When her brother Jarvis and his fiancée Janice visit, Frankie decides that she will go away with the bride and groom after the wedding. Her brother and his bride will give her identity. Frankie says, "They are the *we* of me." Berenice also knows the importance of belonging and love as she remembers her special love for Ludie Freeman. Frankie's frustrations are reflected in Berenice's brother Honey, a young black man who is about to explode. Reality closes in at the end of the play, but Frankie remains unchanged. She still must create dream relationships to meet her emotional needs. *The Member of the Wedding* is a strong psychological classic of the modern American theater.

The Chosen
by Chaim Potok

The Chosen is drawn from the author's boyhood and recounts the experience of growing up as an orthodox Jew in America during the turbulent 1940s. Reuven Malter and Danny Saunders come from different Jewish backgrounds. Reuven's father believes that the Jews must work through the political process to establish a homeland. Danny's father is the leader of the Hasidim, a supremely conservative group who believe that the Jews' only salvation lies in the Torah. Danny has been chosen at birth to be the tzaddik, the leader of his people. Yet his brilliant mind craves much more knowledge than can be had in the narrow confines of his sect. Through a baseball accident, Danny and Reuven become friends. Danny and Reuven find the way to maturity amid the turmoil created in the Jewish community as the state of Israel is born. The author contrasts Danny's remote father, who brings his son up "in silence," with Reuven's father who has a loving closeness with his son. *The Chosen* presents the conflict between faith and intellect while showing a fine picture of Jewish belief and practice.

The Catcher in the Rye
by J.D. Salinger

Holden Caulfield is a prep school adolescent who seeks to shock by sensational actions and vulgar language. The real Holden hides from a reality which he cannot face. He is closest to his little sister Phoebe in a struggle to cope with his brother's death. In a world filled with "phonies," Holden becomes the most pathetic "phoney" of them all, as he struggles to protect himself from what he cannot face. Holden's weekend odyssey around New York City does not help him to mature. He hides in the museum, where things always remain the same. The journey ends at a carousel in Central Park. The author's fine use of first person point of view gives this novel a significant place in the fiction of a young man's struggles to grow up.

Shane
by Jack Schaefer

Bob Starrett and his family are struggling farmers in the western territory of the 1890s. Into their lives rides the courteous and mysterious man Shane, who owns a gun but does not wear it. When Fletcher, the neighboring large ranch owner, tries to drive the small farmers from their homes, Bob's father is forced to stand and fight for his land and his family. The final confrontation comes between Shane and Wilson, who is Fletcher's hired gunman. *Shane* presents the excitement of the West and the noble cowboy hero as seen through the eyes of a small boy.

The Odd Couple
by Neil Simon

This classic comedy pairs Oscar Madison, the slob, with Felix Unger, the neatness maniac. When Felix's poker buddies fear the distraught man will commit suicide, Oscar takes pity on Felix and asks Felix to move in. Comic chaos results as Oscar and Felix begin to influence each other. Witty dialogue and fast-moving action make this play light reading. The play comes to a climax as the two roommates compete for the attentions of the Pigeon sisters, who live upstairs. *The Odd Couple* is a fine example of modern comic technique.

Rabbit, Run
by John Updike

Harry "Rabbit" Angstrom is a forty-year-old adult who cannot cope. Having had his moment of greatness as a high school basketball star, Rabbit spends the rest of his life running away. He leaves his wife Janice and his two children and moves in with Ruth Leonard. After abandoning Ruth, he returns to Janice. Rabbit's irresponsibility increases his wife's drinking and leads to the tragic death of his daughter. Yet, at the end of the novel, Rabbit is still running. Updike's character is a likeable but pathetic man who constantly needs to prove his manhood, but cannot face the obligations that manhood represents. Containing specific descriptive passages, *Rabbit, Run* is a powerful novel of personal failure which would be suitable for more mature readers.

Macho
by Edmund Villasenor

Macho is a powerful novel of the American Chicano community. Roberto is a Mexican youth who struggles to help his family survive. Roberto is lured north by promises of great money to be made working in the United States. Juan Anguilar, an experienced *norteno* or border crosser, becomes Roberto's patron. Together they plan to cross the border *a la brava*, as illegal immigrants. After being defrauded by men who promised to issue entry papers, Juan and Roberto almost die as they attempt to cross the border in a locked van. They eventually find work in the California lettuce fields, but refuse to join the efforts of Chavez and his union. Roberto falls in love with Lydia. He must leave his love, however, to return to Mexico and uphold the family honor by settling an old score with his enemy. *Macho* presents clearly the problems faced by Chicano immigrants as the reader follows Roberto's development from a boy into a man.

Name _____ Date _____

When the Legends Die by Hal Borland

In the numbered blanks at the left, write the letter of the matching person or place.

_____	1.	Taught her son the crafts and customs of his people
_____	2.	Told Tom to recover from his injuries by eating, sleeping, and walking
_____	3.	Tom's roommate
_____	4.	Put Tom to work herding sheep
_____	5.	Site of the country's largest rodeo
_____	6.	Store owner who recognized the quality of Tom's work
_____	7.	Was trained to take fake falls in rodeo competition
_____	8.	Man that Tom's father killed
_____	9.	Tom's childhood home in the wilderness
_____	10.	Offered love which Tom could not accept
_____	11.	Indian who sold his people to the white man
_____	12.	Nickname given because of a rider's violence
_____	13.	Tom's tribe and language
_____	14.	Town near the reservation
_____	15.	Made huge profits by placing crooked bets on Tom's riding ability
_____	16.	Tried to help Tom learn English
_____	17.	Paid Blue Elk to bring Tom to school
_____	18.	Attempted to discipline Tom so he would learn the white man's ways
_____	19.	Name that Tom gave himself
_____	20.	Old man who had an identity with the land

A. Blue Elk
B. Ute
C. Frank No Deer
D. Bald Mountain
E. Jim Thatcher
F. Bear's Brother
G. Luther Spotted Dog
H. Rowena Ellis
I. Benny Grayback
J. Red Dillon
K. Meo
L. Albert Left Hand
M. Bessie
N. Tom
O. Killer Tom Black
P. Madison Square Garden
Q. Mary Redmond
R. Pagosa
S. Agent
T. Dr. Ferguson

Name _____ Date _____

When the Legends Die by Hal Borland

Answer each of the following questions in two or three complete sentences.

1. In what ways was Blue Elk a traitor to all Indians?

    _____

    _____

    _____

    _____

2. How does Tom become brother to the bear after his parents die? Why does Tom later send the bear away?

    _____

    _____

    _____

    _____

3. Why does Tom allow Red Dillon to control him? How does Tom finally break that control?

    _____

    _____

    _____

    _____

4. Why is Tom so violent as a rodeo rider?

    _____

    _____

    _____

    _____

5. Why can Tom not accept the love and companionship that Mary wants to give him?

    _____

    _____

    _____

    _____

Challenge

Write an essay discussing the ways that Tom Black Bull lost his identity as an Indian, and the steps by which he again found that identity.

©1986, 1991 J. Weston Walch, Publisher

Great Books for Independent Reading

Name _____ Date _____

Jane Eyre by Charlotte Brontë

In the numbered blanks at the left, write the letter of the matching person or place.

_____	1.	A mysterious servant
_____	2.	Mr. Rochester's ward
_____	3.	Beautiful and conceited
_____	4.	Saves Jane from death
_____	5.	Runs away from Thornfield
_____	6.	Old faithful family servant
_____	7.	Insane woman who dies in a fire
_____	8.	Intelligent, concerned sisters
_____	9.	Eventually marries Jane
_____	10.	Dies of tuberculosis
_____	11.	Jane's only friend at Gateshead
_____	12.	Jane's legal guardian when she was a child
_____	13.	Stern, hypocritical clergyman
_____	14.	Wise, compassionate teacher
_____	15.	Housekeeper at Thornfield
_____	16.	Jane's selfish cousins
_____	17.	Place where Jane taught school
_____	18.	Adele's mother
_____	19.	Home of Jane's uncle
_____	20.	Where Jane lives at the end of the novel

A. Helen Burns
B. Adele
C. Diana and Mary
D. Rochester
E. Blanche
F. Bertha
G. St. John Rivers
H. Jane
I. Hannah
J. Grace Poole
K. Celene
L. Mrs. Reed
M. Miss Temple
N. Mr. Brocklehurst
O. Eliza and Georgianna
P. Ferndean
Q. Bessie
R. Morton
S. Mrs. Fairfax
T. Madeira

Name _____ Date _____

Jane Eyre by Charlotte Brontë

Answer each of the following questions in two or three complete sentences.

1. Why would Jane's first attempt to marry Rochester not have been legal?

2. What were the difficulties that Jane encountered as she fled from Thornfield?

3. What does Rivers want Jane to do? Why does she refuse?

4. What had happened to Thornfield and to Rochester during Jane's absence?

5. State in your own words two of the important themes in *Jane Eyre*.

Challenge

Why has *Jane Eyre* been considered one of the first important novels to make an important statement about the equality of the sexes?

©1986, 1991 J. Weston Walch, Publisher

Great Books for Independent Reading

Name _____ Date _____

Great Expectations by Charles Dickens

In the numbered blanks at the left, write the letter of the matching person or place.

_____ 1. The pub in Pip's village

_____ 2. Learns to love through experiencing suffering

_____ 3. The pale young gentleman

_____ 4. Attempts to kill Pip out on the marshes

_____ 5. Estella's mother

_____ 6. Pip's benefactor

_____ 7. Was married to Wemmick

_____ 8. Is married to Joe at the end of the novel

_____ 9. Wanted to claim credit for Pip's good fortune

_____ 10. Miss Havisham's deceitful half-brother

_____ 11. Pip's lodgings in London

_____ 12. Lawyer who became Pip's guardian

_____ 13. Lived with The Aged in his "Castle"

_____ 14. Wanted to hurt others as she had been hurt

_____ 15. Decaying old mansion

_____ 16. Deserted his bride on their wedding day

_____ 17. Pip's boyhood home

_____ 18. Fine example of simple, honest goodness

_____ 19. Estella's first husband

_____ 20. Pip's sister

A. Miss Skiffins
B. Wemmick
C. Orlick
D. Satis House
E. Jolly Bargeman
F. The Forge
G. Barnard's Inn
H. Magwitch
I. Drummele
J. Pumblechook
K. Mrs. Joe
L. Miss Havisham
M. Biddy
N. Joe
O. Herbert
P. Molly
Q. Jaggers
R. Estella
S. Compeyson
T. Arthur

Name _____ Date _____

Great Expectations by Charles Dickens

Answer each of the following questions in two or three complete sentences.

1. How does Pip's childhood encounter with the convict affect him?

    _____

    _____

    _____

    _____

2. How does Joe try to help Pip when Pip is a child?

    _____

    _____

    _____

    _____

3. Why does spending time at Miss Havisham's make Pip dissatisfied with his life?

    _____

    _____

    _____

    _____

4. In what ways does Pip become spoiled and selfish after he goes to London?

    _____

    _____

    _____

    _____

5. How do Pip's experiences after the arrival of Magwitch contribute to Pip's growth and maturity?

    _____

    _____

    _____

    _____

Challenge

Great Expectations is a fine character study in Pip's growth from childhood innocence to mature adulthood. Write an essay tracing the important phases in this change. Support your statements by listing some of the specific events which cause these changes to occur.

Name _____   Date _____

The Summer of My German Soldier by Bette Greene

In the numbered blanks at the left, write the letter of the matching person or place.

_____ 1. Known as the prettiest girl in town

_____ 2. Location of the prison camp

_____ 3. Patty's grandfather

_____ 4. Made Patty feel that she was really a person of value

_____ 5. Location of the reform school

_____ 6. Newspaper reporter who tried to help Patty

_____ 7. Had a cruel and abusive father

_____ 8. Worked in Bergen's department store

_____ 9. Tried to be the mother that Patty needed

_____ 10. Transported Patty to reform school

_____ 11. Always felt inferior to his wife's family

_____ 12. Ruth's son

_____ 13. Got Patty into trouble by throwing rocks at cars

_____ 14. Patty's neurotic, self-centered mother

_____ 15. Headmistress of the reform school

_____ 16. Richest man in Jenkinsville

_____ 17. FBI agent who questioned Patty

_____ 18. Tried to give Patty love by buying her things

_____ 19. Patty's lawyer

_____ 20. Patty's adorable younger sister

A. Jenkinsville
B. Ruth
C. Harry Bergen
D. Sharon
E. Patty
F. Anton Reiker
G. Pearl
H. J.G. Jackson
I. Samuel Fried
J. Grandma Fried
K. Sister Parker
L. Robert
M. Charlene Madlee
N. Freddy
O. Edna Louise
P. Pierce
Q. Calvin Grimes
R. Mr. Kishner
S. Bolton
T. Miss Laud

©1986, 1991 J. Weston Walch, Publisher

Great Books for Independent Reading

Name _____ Date _____

The Summer of My German Soldier by Bette Greene

Answer each of the following questions in two or three complete sentences.

1. How do Patty's interests and feelings show her to be a special, sensitive person?

    _____

    _____

    _____

    _____

2. In what ways is Patty a victim of family circumstances for which she is not responsible?

    _____

    _____

    _____

    _____

3. Why does being Jewish create problems for Patty?

    _____

    _____

    _____

    _____

4. Why is Patty's relationship with Anton so special?

    _____

    _____

    _____

    _____

5. Explain the meaning of Ruth's statement: "You've got yourself some irregular second folks, and you've been paying more 'n top dollar for them. So jest don't go a-wishing for what ain't nevah gonna be" (p. 192).

    _____

    _____

    _____

    _____

Challenge

Developing characters are those who change and grow throughout the progress of a novel. Discuss the ways in which Patty's experiences have made her a stronger person. Why is she indeed, "a beginning swimmer who will make it to shore" (p. 199)?

Name _____   Date _____

Tex by S.E. Hinton

Place a (+) before each statement that is true and a (0) before each statement that is false.

_____ 1. Tex is a junior in high school.

_____ 2. Tex and Johnny Collins share a mutual love of horses.

_____ 3. Mason had to sell the horses to get money for the brothers to live on.

_____ 4. Mason hoped to get into college on a football scholarship.

_____ 5. The boys have heard from their father regularly.

_____ 6. Tex frequently has nightmares about the death of his mother.

_____ 7. Cole Collins blames Mason for Johnny's getting drunk.

_____ 8. Tex is arrested for shoplifting in a clothing store.

_____ 9. Lem Peters is dealing in drugs so he can support his wife and child.

_____ 10. Mason and Tex become heroes when they single-handedly capture two escaped convicts.

_____ 11. Pop is able to buy Negrito back for Tex.

_____ 12. Tex's favorite member of the school faculty is Coach McCollough.

_____ 13. When Johnny and Tex quarrel, Jamie wants to get the boys to be friends again.

_____ 14. Pop is very angry when Mrs. Johnson calls him about Tex's school pranks.

_____ 15. Tex learns from a statement of Mason's that Pop is not his real father.

_____ 16. Lem Peters accidently shoots Tex in the chest.

_____ 17. After he is injured, Tex telephones Mason.

_____ 18. Tex had been born while Pop was in prison.

_____ 19. Jamie tells Tex at the end of the story that she is willing to marry him.

_____ 20. At the end of the novel, Mason has given up his plans for college.

Name _____ Date _____

Tex by S.E. Hinton

Answer each of the following questions in two or three complete sentences.

1. What does Tex mean when he says that he is a "stayer," and Mason is a "goer"?

_____

_____

_____

_____

2. Although the brothers fight frequently, how does the author show the reader that Mason and Tex love each other?

_____

_____

_____

_____

3. Why is Tex so confused about his feelings for Jamie Collins?

_____

_____

_____

_____

4. Why does Tex say that the dead convict reminds Tex of himself?

_____

_____

_____

_____

5. What happens to Tex when he runs away from the school with Lem Peters?

_____

_____

_____

_____

Challenge

Write an essay discussing the choices made by the characters in *Tex*. Which characters make choices which will probably yield positive results? Which characters make choices which will probably lead to trouble?

©1986, 1991 J. Weston Walch, Publisher

Great Books for Independent Reading

Name _____   Date _____

The Metamorphosis by Franz Kafka

Correctly complete each sentence with information from the novel.

1. Gregor Samsa works as _____.

2. Gregor's greatest fear about his work is that _____.

3. When he becomes an insect, Gregor's physical difficulties include _____
    and _____.

4. The person that Gregor fears most is _____.

5. Gregor is finally able to open the locked door of his room by _____
    _____.

6. The person who reacts most violently to the change in Gregor is _____.

7. The first time Gregor leaves his room, his father injures him by _____.

8. The family member who tries to help and feed Gregor is _____.

9. Gregor had to support his family financially after _____.

10. Gregor finds his room more comfortable when _____.

11. Physical changes which take place in Gregor over a period of time include _____
    _____.

12. The kind of motion that Gregor enjoys most is _____.

13. Because Gregor cannot work, to gain income the family _____.

14. Gregor's chief contact with his family comes through _____.

15. The father attempts to kill Gregor by _____.

16. The figure of Death is represented in the story by _____.

17. Gregor is drawn from his room by the sound of _____.

18. When the lodgers see Gregor, they _____.

19. After his death, Gregor's body is disposed of by _____.

20. After Gregor's death, the rest of the family expresses freedom by _____
    _____.

Great Books for Independent Reading

Name _____ Date _____

The Metamorphosis by Franz Kafka

Answer each of the following questions in two or three complete sentences.

1. What positive traits, as a family member and a workman, does Gregor Samsa possess?

   _____

   _____

   _____

   _____

2. Why does he fear the chief clerk?

   _____

   _____

   _____

   _____

3. Why is the reaction of others to Gregor's situation both unfair and illogical?

   _____

   _____

   _____

   _____

4. How is Gregor rejected every time he tries to communicate with the other members of his family?

   _____

   _____

   _____

   _____

5. How does Gregor deteriorate mentally from his metamorphosis until his death?

   _____

   _____

   _____

   _____

Challenge

Kafka presents an absurd plot, with a very vital theme: the struggle of the individual to find meaning in life and personal relationships. Discuss the ways in which Gregor struggles for this meaning, and the reasons that he fails to find any meaning at all.

Name _____ Date _____

A Separate Peace by John Knowles

Correctly complete each sentence with information from the novel.

1. Gene begins his story when he returns to _____ about _____ years after the main action of the novel.

2. Phineas got away with breaking rules because he had a marvelous ability to _____ _____.

3. Phineas says that his pink shirt is a symbol of _____.

4. Membership in the Suicide Society of the Summer Session involved _____ _____.

5. The game Phineas invented was called _____.

6. Phineas said that the war had been invented by _____.

7. Gene and Phineas skip school and spend the night _____.

8. Gene is angry because he knows that Phineas had tried to wreck _____ _____.

9. Phineas falls out of the tree because _____.

10. Dr. Stanpole says that Phineas will _____ but will never be able to _____.

11. When he goes to visit Phineas at home, Gene tells Phineas that _____ _____.

12. Gene takes a job as crew manager to _____.

13. In Phineas' absence, leadership in school affairs is taken over by _____.

14. When Phineas returns, he makes Gene begin to _____.

15. To help the war effort, the Devon students _____ and _____.

16. The first boy to enlist from Devon is _____.

17. Brinker calls a night meeting to _____.

18. The only witness to Phineas' accident was _____.

19. Phineas dies when _____.

20. Phineas had to pretend that the war did not exist because _____ _____.

Name _____   Date _____

A *Separate Peace* by John Knowles

Answer each of the following questions in two or three complete sentences.

1. When Gene returns to his old school, what things seem different? What things seem the same?

    _____

    _____

    _____

    _____

2. Contrast the personalities of Gene and Phineas.

    _____

    _____

    _____

    _____

3. How does Gene try to relieve his guilt feelings about Phineas' accident?

    _____

    _____

    _____

    _____

4. Why is Leper a real "casualty" of the war?

    _____

    _____

    _____

    _____

5. How does Phineas respond to the accusations made against Gene?

    _____

    _____

    _____

    _____

Challenge

Write an essay explaining Gene's statement (p. 255): "My war ended before I ever put on a uniform; I was on active duty all my time at school; I killed my enemy there."

Name _____ Date _____

Christy by Catherine Marshall

In the numbered blanks at the left, write the letter of the matching person or place.

_____ 1. Was unsure of his calling to be a minister

_____ 2. Mailman, Christy's escort to the Cove

_____ 3. Had an idiot son

_____ 4. Had once been Bird's Eye's sweetheart

_____ 5. Christy's home town

_____ 6. Shot Tom McHone in the back

_____ 7. Had been raped by a man whom she trusted

_____ 8. Most gentle and sensitive of the mountain women

_____ 9. Housekeeper at the Mission

_____ 10. Challenged David at the "working" with a gun

_____ 11. Learned from Christy how to be a more attractive woman

_____ 12. Introduced Christy to the idea of the Danish Folk Schools

_____ 13. Hired Christy to teach in Cutter Gap

_____ 14. Was saved when Dr. MacNeill operated

_____ 15. Proud owner of a pet raccoon

_____ 16. Native of the Cove who returned to help his own people

_____ 17. Old lady who died in peace and confidence

_____ 18. Was recalled to life by the power of love

_____ 19. Miss Alice's daughter

_____ 20. Businessman who helped to supply the Mission with needed books and equipment

A. Asheville
B. Mr. Pentland
C. Dr. Ferrand
D. Miss Ida
E. Creed Allen
F. Ruby Mae
G. Hazen Smith
H. Lundy Taylor
I. Margaret MacNeill
J. Fairlight Spencer
K. Opal McHone
L. Christy
M. David Grantland
N. Aunt Polly Teague
O. Miss Alice
P. Dr. MacNeill
Q. Bird's Eye Taylor
R. Mrs. Browning
S. Little Burl Allen
T. Mrs. O'Teale

Name _____   Date _____

Christy by Catherine Marshall

Answer each of the following questions in two or three complete sentences.

1. What were Christy's motives for going to Cutter Gap?

    _____
    _____
    _____
    _____

2. What were some of the difficulties that Christy faced in her teaching?

    _____
    _____
    _____
    _____

3. What were some of the character traits and prejudices of the people of Cutter Gap?

    _____
    _____
    _____
    _____

4. How was the religion practiced by Miss Alice Henderson different from the religion of most of the Cove people?

    _____
    _____
    _____
    _____

5. Why did David Grantland have problems with his parishioners? Why was David unsure of his own role with these people?

    _____
    _____
    _____
    _____

Challenge

What specific experiences helped Christy Huddleston grow from an immature schoolgirl into a mature young woman?

Name _____ Date _____

The Heart is a Lonely Hunter by Carson McCullers

Place a (+) before each statement that is true and a (0) before each statement that is false.

_____ 1. Singer did most of the cooking for Antonapoulous and himself.

_____ 2. Antonapoulous was committed to a mental institution by his cousin.

_____ 3. Mick's father had been a railroad worker before he was injured.

_____ 4. Mick took care of her two younger brothers.

_____ 5. Biff Brannon got a job as handyman with a carnival.

_____ 6. Mick was the only girl in her family.

_____ 7. Doctor Copeland's daughter worked as a waitress in Biff's restaurant.

_____ 8. Mick's greatest passion in life was music.

_____ 9. Singer rarely attempted to really talk with anyone after Antonapoulous left.

_____ 10. Portia's husband was sent to jail for knifing a man.

_____ 11. Doctor Copeland was himself seriously ill.

_____ 12. Mick's brother Ralph shot Baby Wilson with a rifle.

_____ 13. At Mick's first party, all of the boys and girls danced easily and had a good time.

_____ 14. Blount and Mick liked to spend time with Singer because Singer was such a good listener.

_____ 15. Singer received a telegram informing him that Antonapoulous had died.

_____ 16. After Mick and Harry spent the day in the woods, Harry offered to marry Mick.

_____ 17. Doctor Copeland committed suicide.

_____ 18. Mick got a job working at Woolworth's.

_____ 19. Brannon decided to close his cafe and move on to a new town.

_____ 20. Willie Copeland died in prison.

©1986, 1991 J. Weston Walch, Publisher

Great Books for Independent Reading

Name _____ Date _____

The Heart is a Lonely Hunter by Carson McCullers

Answer each of the following questions in two or three complete sentences.

1. What did Mick mean by her "inside room" and her "outside room"?

    _____

    _____

    _____

    _____

2. Why did each of the four main characters enjoy spending time with Singer?

    _____

    _____

    _____

    _____

3. How does Dr. Copeland try to help his people?

    _____

    _____

    _____

    _____

4. How does Biff change after Alice's death?

    _____

    _____

    _____

    _____

5. How has Mick Kelley grown up by the end of the novel?

    _____

    _____

    _____

    _____

Challenge

Write an essay explaining how each character in the novel is a "lonely hunter." What is each one seeking? How is Singer important to each one's search?

Great Books for Independent Reading

Name _____ Date _____

The Member of the Wedding by Carson McCullers

Select the letter of the word or phrase which correctly completes each statement.

_____ 1. Berenice is described as all of the following except: (A) blind in one eye (B) slender (C) loving and affectionate (D) the family cook.

_____ 2. Frankie's mother (A) works in a jewelry store (B) is very active socially (C) died when Frankie was born (D) doesn't want Frankie and John Henry to play together.

_____ 3. Jarvis (A) is older than Frankie (B) is engaged (C) is in the army (D) all of the above.

_____ 4. Frankie's tendency to fantasize is shown by (A) her desire to belong to a club (B) her relationship with John Henry (C) writing and acting in plays (D) her desire to be helpful to Berenice.

_____ 5. Frankie's greatest desire in life is (A) to be pretty (B) to be married (C) to be intelligent (D) to belong and to be loved.

_____ 6. Frankie's greatest source of anxiety is (A) her weight (B) her height (C) her name (D) her dirty elbows.

_____ 7. The other character whose feelings most closely resemble Frankie's feelings is (A) T.T. (B) John Henry (C) Honey (D) Sis Laura.

_____ 8. Frankie is absolutely convinced that she will (A) marry Barney McKean (B) never amount to anything (C) be able to go with Janice and Jarvis (D) become a concert pianist.

_____ 9. Frankie's father (A) is a jeweler (B) doesn't understand Frankie (C) gives Frankie permission to go shopping by herself (D) all of the above.

_____ 10. Berenice says that all of her husbands and boyfriends (A) reminded her of Ludie (B) were small pieces of Ludie (C) were different from Ludie (D) gave her as much happiness as Ludie had given her.

_____ 11. The clothes that Frankie buys for the wedding (A) are totally inappropriate (B) could easily be exchanged (C) were picked out by Berenice (D) were very attractive and suitable.

_____ 12. After the wedding ceremony, (A) Frankie goes with Janice and Jarvis (B) Berenice finds another job (C) Frankie has to be dragged from the car (D) Mr. Addams becomes seriously ill.

_____ 13. The death of Sis Laura foreshadows (looks ahead to) (A) the wedding (B) the death of John Henry (C) the departure of Janice and Jarvis (D) the death of Ludie.

_____ 14. Act One ends with (A) the wedding ceremony (B) the singing of a Negro spiritual (C) John Henry's death (D) a real change in Frankie's personality.

_____ 15. Honey dies when (A) he is shot (B) he is cut by a razor (C) he is trying to run from the police (D) he commits suicide in jail.

_____ 16. When she cannot go with her brother and his bride, Frankie (A) tries to run away (B) tries to kill herself (C) blames her father (D) faints.

_____ 17. The character in the play who has the best grasp of reality is (A) Mr. Addams (B) John Henry (C) Berenice (D) Jarvis.

_____ 18. At the end of the play, Frankie has transferred her fantasies to (A) Mary and Barney (B) the movies (C) the girls next door (D) John Henry.

_____ 19. In the final scene, the family (A) is going to John Henry's funeral (B) is leaving town (C) is moving to a different house (D) is planning a vacation.

_____ 20. The author's main theme in this play is (A) the importance of marriage (B) racial tensions in the South (C) the need for belonging (D) the problems of neglected children.

©1986, 1991 J. Weston Walch, Publisher

Great Books for Independent Reading

Name _____ Date _____

The Member of the Wedding by Carson McCullers

Answer each of the following questions in two or three complete sentences.

1. Explain Frankie's statement regarding Janice and Jarvis: "They are the we of me."

    _____

    _____

    _____

    _____

2. What episodes in the play most clearly show Frankie's need to belong?

    _____

    _____

    _____

    _____

3. How is Berenice a mother figure to Frankie and John Henry?

    _____

    _____

    _____

    _____

4. How does Berenice say that her feelings for T.T. differ from the feelings that she had had for Ludie?

    _____

    _____

    _____

    _____

5. What problems do Frankie and Honey have in common?

    _____

    _____

    _____

    _____

Challenge

A developing character in literature is one who changes and learns from experience. A static character shows no change at all. Is Frankie Addams a developing character or a static character? Support your answer with evidence from the play.

Great Books for Independent Reading

Name _____   Date _____

The Chosen by Chaim Potok

In the numbered blanks at the left, write the letter of the matching person, place, or thing.

_____ 1. Danny's choice for graduate school

_____ 2. Narrator of the novel

_____ 3. Danny's younger brother

_____ 4. Jewish sacred scriptures

_____ 5. Group that supported the establishment of a Jewish political state in Israel

_____ 6. Complicated verbal quiz used by Danny's father to show off his brilliant son to his congregation

_____ 7. Rabbi or leader

_____ 8. Hebrew secondary school

_____ 9. Had a photographic memory

_____ 10. Deliverer that the Jews believed would come

_____ 11. Spoken Hebrew language of European Jews

_____ 12. Blind boy that Reuven meets in the hospital

_____ 13. Mystical orthodox Jewish sect which began in Eastern Europe

_____ 14. Where Reuven and Danny went to college together

_____ 15. Brought his son up "in silence"

_____ 16. Non-Jews

_____ 17. Complicated text for Hebrew religious and philosophical studies

_____ 18. Helped Danny select his reading material at the public library

_____ 19. Important German psychiatrist

_____ 20. Danny and Reuven's college professor of Talmud

A. Reuven Malter
B. Danny Saunders
C. Reb Malter
D. Reb Saunders
E. Talmud
F. Yeshiva
G. Billy
H. Hasidim
I. Levi
J. Zionists
K. Messiah
L. Tzaddik
M. Freud
N. Goyim
O. Torah
P. Hirsh
Q. Reb Gershenson
R. Columbia
S. Yiddish
T. Gematriya

Name _____ Date _____

The Chosen by Chaim Potok

Answer each of the following questions in two or three complete sentences.

1. Describe the circumstances under which Danny and Reuven become friends.

    _____

    _____

    _____

    _____

2. How is Danny's relationship with his father different from Reuven's relationship with his father?

    _____

    _____

    _____

    _____

3. In what ways is Danny Saunders a very special person? Why does he rebel against the life that his father has planned for him?

    _____

    _____

    _____

    _____

4. What is the cause of the conflict between Reb Malter and Reb Saunders when the state of Israel is established?

    _____

    _____

    _____

    _____

5. Why did Reb Saunders choose to bring up Danny "in silence"?

    _____

    _____

    _____

    _____

Challenge

Reb Saunders says that Danny will be "a tzaddik to the world." Write an essay discussing what Saunders means by this statement. How have Danny's education and upbringing prepared the young man for this very special role?

Great Books for Independent Reading

Name _____   Date _____

The Catcher in the Rye by J.D. Salinger

In the numbered blanks at the left, write the letter of the matching person or place.

_____ 1. Boy who died by jumping from the window of his dorm room

_____ 2. Girl that Holden took to a play

_____ 3. Last school from which Holden was expelled

_____ 4. The place where everything always stayed the same

_____ 5. History teacher at Pencey Prep

_____ 6. Piano player in a Greenwich Village bar

_____ 7. Pseudonym that Phoebe used for writing stories

_____ 8. Prostitute who visited Holden in his hotel room

_____ 9. Holden's younger brother who had died of leukemia

_____ 10. Boy with bad breath and pimples

_____ 11. English teacher who destroys Holden's last illusions about adults

_____ 12. The one person that Holden is really close to

_____ 13. Girl that Holden had dated briefly one summer

_____ 14. Location of the carousel with the gold ring

_____ 15. Beats up Holden for not paying

_____ 16. A corporation lawyer

_____ 17. Used to give the younger boys lectures on sex

_____ 18. Student whose mother Holden meets on the train

_____ 19. Holden's roommate at Pencey

_____ 20. Holden's older brother who works in Hollywood

A. Sunny
B. Mr. Caulfield
C. Central Park
D. Mr. Antolini
E. Museum of Natural History
F. James Castle
G. Hazel Weatherfield
H. Carl Luce
I. Ernie
J. Phoebe
K. Ernest Morrow
L. Sally Hayes
M. Maurice
N. Stradtlater
O. Ackely
P. D.B.
Q. Allie
R. Mr. Spencer
S. Jane Gallagher
T. Pencey Prep

Name _____ Date _____

The Catcher in the Rye by J.D Salinger

Answer each of the following questions in two or three complete sentences.

1. Why has Holden been a misfit in every school that he has attended?

    _____

    _____

    _____

    _____

2. How is Holden's relationship with Jane Gallagher different from his relationship with Sally Hayes?

    _____

    _____

    _____

    _____

3. How do you know that Holden was deeply affected by the death of his brother?

    _____

    _____

    _____

    _____

4. Why is Holden able to be honest with his younger sister?

    _____

    _____

    _____

    _____

5. Why does Holden like the museum and the zoo?

    _____

    _____

    _____

    _____

Challenge

How does Holden Caulfield, by becoming the biggest phoney of all, create a fantasy world to protect himself from a reality that he cannot face?

Name _____   Date _____

Shane by Jack Schaefer

In the numbered blanks at the left, write the letter of the matching person or place. You will use some letters more than once.

_____ 1. Was hit on the head to prevent his being involved in a fight

_____ 2. Rancher who intended to drive the small farmers from the valley

_____ 3. Boy who tells the story

_____ 4. Tried to beat Shane up by having two of his men hold Shane down

_____ 5. Came and offered to work for Bob's father after Shane left

_____ 6. Man to whom the farmers looked for leadership

_____ 7. Wanted the house in the West painted like a house in New England

_____ 8. Rode out of the valley after his job was done

_____ 9. Gunfighter hired to drive the small farmers from their land

_____ 10. Unorganized western land where the story takes place

_____ 11. Farmer who saw the new gunfighter arrive in town

_____ 12. Had his arm broken in a fight with Shane

_____ 13. Refused Fletcher's offer of a job as his foreman

_____ 14. Recognized that the family's roots had been planted deep into the soil by Shane

_____ 15. Tried to shoot Shane from a saloon balcony

_____ 16. Fletcher's foreman who was badly beaten by Shane

_____ 17. The first small farmer who was killed

_____ 18. Owner of the local store and saloon

_____ 19. Only wore his gun when he intended to use it

_____ 20. Made the best apple pies in the territory

A. Bob Starrett
B. Joe Starrett
C. Shane
D. Grafton
E. Fletcher
F. Ernie Wright
G. Morgan
H. Chris
I. Territory
J. Marian
K. Johnson
L. Wilson

Great Books for Independent Reading

Name _____   Date _____

Shane by Jack Schaefer

Answer each of the following questions in two or three complete sentences.

1. Why did Shane decide to remain with the Starretts?

2. What actions of Shane's made him seem mysterious to the family?

3. What did Shane mean when he told Bob that a gun was a tool?

4. How did Marian show her support for her husband?

5. How did Shane take care of both Wilson and Fletcher in one fight?

Challenge

Write a newspaper article describing the events of the final showdown from the time that Shane entered the saloon until he left. Explain how a third-person observer, one who was not emotionally involved in the action, would have seen the fight.

©1986, 1991 J. Weston Walch, Publisher

Great Books for Independent Reading

Name _____ Date _____

The Odd Couple by Neil Simon

Correctly complete each sentence with information from the play.

1. As the play opens, the poker players are concerned because _____
_____.

2. By profession, Oscar Madison is _____.

3. The general condition of Oscar's apartment at the beginning of the play may best be described as _____.

4. Instead of a suicide note, Felix sent his wife _____.

5. Felix's feelings about himself may be best described as _____
_____.

6. Oscar offers to let Felix _____.

7. For the poker party in Act II, Felix has prepared _____.

8. The other poker players envy Oscar and Felix because _____.

9. Felix and Oscar have spent most of their evenings _____.

10. Oscar first met the Pigeon sisters _____.

11. On the night of the dinner party, Felix is very upset because Oscar _____
_____.

12. The elaborate dinner that Felix had planned _____.

13. Felix gets the sympathy of the Pigeon sisters by _____.

14. The girls invite Felix and Oscar _____.

15. At the end of Act II, Felix refuses _____
_____.

16. At the beginning of Act III, Oscar deliberately _____.

17. Oscar has made a typewritten list of _____.

18. Oscar orders Felix to _____.

19. Before Felix leaves he makes Oscar _____.

20. At the end of the play, Felix _____.

Name _____ Date _____

The Odd Couple by Neil Simon

Answer each of the following questions in two or three complete sentences.

1. Why are Felix's poker buddies very concerned about him?

    _____

    _____

    _____

    _____

2. In what ways does Oscar's personality directly contrast with Felix's?

    _____

    _____

    _____

    _____

3. How does the appearance of the set change from the opening of Act I to the opening of Act II?

    _____

    _____

    _____

    _____

4. What habits of Felix's annoy Oscar the most?

    _____

    _____

    _____

5. How does Felix win with the Pigeon sisters, while Oscar fails?

    _____

    _____

    _____

    _____

Challenge

Write an essay describing the ways that Oscar and Felix change each other during the time that the two men live together. What indications are there that Felix has the stronger personality of the two?

Name _____ Date _____

Rabbit, Run by John Updike

Select the letter of the word or phrase which correctly completes the sentence.

———— 1. The boys playing basketball in the opening scene of the novel remind Rabbit of (A) his son (B) his own high school greatness (C) his dead hopes for a professional sports career (D) his job selling sports equipment.

———— 2. When the story opens, Rabbit is working (A) as a coach (B) at a gas station (C) as a used-car salesman (D) demonstrating kitchen gadgets.

———— 3. Rabbit's age is about (A) 40 (B) 20 (C) 30 (D) 50.

———— 4. Rabbit's wife Janice (A) is an alcoholic (B) is pregnant (C) escapes into the fantasy world of television (D) all of the above.

———— 5. When Rabbit first begins to run away, he thinks he will head for (A) Boston (B) Europe (C) Florida (D) Philadelphia.

———— 6. Rabbit is introduced to Ruth Leonard by (A) his sister, Mim (B) Coach Tothero (C) Reverend Eccles (D) Janice's mother.

———— 7. Rabbit enjoys being with Ruth because (A) she makes him feel completely masculine (B) he has no responsibility for her (C) she does not demand that he marry her (D) all of the above.

———— 8. Rabbit's first name is (A) Harry (B) Nelson (C) Jack (D) William.

———— 9. Rabbit lives with Ruth for about (A) a year (B) two weeks (C) a month (D) six months.

———— 10. Reverend Eccles tries to help Rabbit (A) learn to accept responsibility (B) find God (C) as a favor to Janice's family (D) because he feels sorry for Rabbit.

———— 11. While living with Ruth, Rabbit works (A) as a janitor (B) as a gardener (C) as a cab driver (D) at nothing at all.

———— 12. Rabbit is most totally at ease with (A) Ruth (B) his son Nelson (C) his father-in-law (D) Reverend Eccles.

———— 13. Rabbit abandons Ruth (A) at Eccles' insistence (B) when his daughter is born (C) when Ruth throws him out (D) when he decides to leave town.

———— 14. Tothero (A) was Rabbit's basketball coach (B) has a stroke (C) comes to offer Rabbit and Janice his sympathy (D) all of the above.

———— 15. Reverend Eccles (A) is a basketball fan (B) has two sons (C) feels inadequate as a minister and as a person (D) has a very homely wife.

———— 16. Janice drowns Rebecca (A) because she can't stand to hear the child's crying (B) because Janice is drunk (C) because Janice wants to hurt Rabbit (D) because Janice doesn't love the child.

———— 17. The baby's death was seen by (A) Nelson (B) no one (C) Janice's mother (D) the next-door neighbor.

———— 18. At his daughter's funeral, Rabbit (A) takes the responsibility for his family (B) runs away again (C) apologizes to Eccles (D) tries to commit suicide.

———— 19. When Rabbit learns that Ruth is pregnant, he (A) offers to marry her (B) is pleased (C) is angry (D) tells her to have an abortion.

———— 20. Rabbit's character traits include all of the following except: (A) a mean, malicious nature (B) an inability to accept responsibility (C) a need to prove his manhood (D) a love of motion.

Name _____ Date _____

Rabbit, Run by John Updike

Answer each of the following questions in two or three complete sentences.

1. How did Rabbit get his nickname? Why does the name suit his personality?

2. In what specific ways does Jack Eccles try to help Rabbit?

3. Why does Rabbit go to Tothero's when he first leaves his wife?

4. Why does Rabbit feel trapped after he goes back to Janice?

5. In what ways is Rabbit responsible for Rebecca's death?

Challenge

A static character does not grow or change through experience. Why is Harry Angstrom such a static character? Cite examples of his behavior at the end of the novel which duplicate his earlier actions.

Name _____ Date _____

Macho by Edmund Villasenor

Place a (+) before each statement that is true and a (0) before each statement that is false.

_____ 1. Roberto was the eldest son in his family.

_____ 2. Roberto's father had been made foreman over many men who were older than he was.

_____ 3. Roberto's employer had no sympathy for Roberto's difficult family situation.

_____ 4. The Nortenos lured the village boys with stories of the great fortunes that were to be made in the United States.

_____ 5. Roberto agreed to give Juan Aguilar half of each day's pay in return for Juan's help and protection.

_____ 6. Roberto's sister is braver and more responsible than any other member of his family.

_____ 7. Pedro was a childhood friend who later became Roberto's enemy.

_____ 8. Juan Aguilar was well liked by all of the other men in Roberto's village.

_____ 9. In Empalme, Roberto and Aguilar are able to buy work permits to allow them to enter the United States.

_____ 10. Aguilar is clever enough to make money off the other men who are waiting to immigrate.

_____ 11. "A la brava" meant illegal entry.

_____ 12. Chavez and his union were trying to persuade the American government to admit a larger Mexican working force into California.

_____ 13. Aguilar prevents Pedro from killing Roberto in a knife fight.

_____ 14. Roberto gets very sick from drinking contaminated water.

_____ 15. Luis Espinoza gets Roberto and Aguilar into California and finds work for them.

_____ 16. Little John is the driver of the truck in which the men almost die of suffocation.

_____ 17. Roberto is amazed at the amount of food provided for the farm workers.

_____ 18. Roberto and Aguilar join the forces of Chavez in a strike against the field management.

_____ 19. Roberto's family becomes very prosperous because of the money Roberto is able to send home.

_____ 20. In the final confrontation of the story, Roberto kills Pedro in a gunfight.

©1986, 1991 J. Weston Walch, Publisher

Great Books for Independent Reading

Name _____   Date _____

Macho by Edmund Villasenor

Answer each of the following questions in two or three complete sentences.

1. Describe the family circumstances which force Roberto to go north.

    _____

    _____

    _____

    _____

2. How is the ignorance of the Mexican workers exploited by the unscrupulous men in the immigration camp?

    _____

    _____

    _____

    _____

3. Describe the relationship which develops between Roberto and Aguilar.

    _____

    _____

    _____

    _____

4. How does Roberto's love for Lydia conflict with his drive for revenge against Pedro?

    _____

    _____

    _____

    _____

5. Why does Roberto leave Lydia and return to his village, even though his sister warns him not to come?

    _____

    _____

    _____

    _____

Challenge

Write an essay describing Roberto's development from a boy into a man. What are some of the experiences that cause him to change?

Great Books for Independent Reading

Answer Keys

When the Legends Die by Hal Borland

OBJECTIVE:

1. M	6. E	11. A	16. H
2. T	7. N	12. O	17. S
3. G	8. C	13. B	18. I
4. L	9. D	14. R	19. F
5. P	10. Q	15. J	20. K

SHORT ANSWER:

1. Tricked his own people, made money by trading the Indian to the white man.
2. Cub's mother dead. Boy and cub fill each other's loneliness. Sends cub away to save bear from being killed.
3. To become a rodeo rider—total world gone, no motivation. Takes Red's money and goes off on his own.
4. Takes out his anger on the animals.
5. Cannot let himself feel love.

CHALLENGE:

Lost meaning on reservation, in school, crooked rodeo system, burning Meo's home. Found by a return to the land and confronting the bear.

Jane Eyre by Charlotte Brontë

OBJECTIVE:

1. J	6. I	11. Q	16. O
2. B	7. F	12. L	17. R
3. E	8. C	13. N	18. K
4. G	9. D	14. M	19. T
5. H	10. A	15. S	20. P

SHORT ANSWER:

1. His first wife was still alive.
2. Rain, hunger, no money, homelessness.
3. Marry him and go to India. She doesn't love him.
4. House burned, Rochester blinded.
5. Equality of all people, importance of individual integrity.

CHALLENGE:

Jane and Rochester as mental equals, her struggle for survival at Lowood against Rivers, final winning of identity.

Great Expectations by Charles Dickens

OBJECTIVE:

1. E	6. H	11. G	16. S
2. R	7. A	12. Q	17. F
3. O	8. M	13. B	18. N
4. C	9. J	14. L	19. I
5. P	10. T	15. D	20. K

ANSWER KEYS (continued)

Great Expectations by Charles Dickens (continued)

SHORT ANSWER:
1. Made him feel afraid and guilty.
2. Defended Pip from Mrs. Joe's temper, tried to give him special treats.
3. Estella made him feel crude, common, and discontented.
4. Spends too much money, cares only for Estella, selfish lifestyle.
5. Helps Magwitch instead of thinking about himself.

CHALLENGE:

Abused child, dissatisfied with life, spoiled young gentleman, rises to meet crisis, learns what real values are.

The Summer of My German Soldier by Bette Greene

OBJECTIVE:

1. O	6. M	11. C	16. H
2. A	7. E	12. L	17. P
3. I	8. K	13. N	18. J
4. F	9. B	14. G	19. R
5. S	10. Q	15. T	20. D

SHORT ANSWER:
1. Desire to be loved and to please, caring for Ruth and Anton.
2. Weak mother, violent, masochistic father.
3. Couldn't go to the summer camp, community violence when they learned that she had hidden a German.
4. He made her feel loved.
5. They will never treat her differently. She must accept things as they are.

CHALLENGE:

Learns to withstand community pressure, to see that she is really a good person, to begin to develop her own goals.

Tex by S.E. Hinton

OBJECTIVE:

1. 0	6. +	11. 0	16. 0
2. 0	7. 0	12. 0	17. 0
3. +	8. 0	13. +	18. +
4. 0	9. +	14. 0	19. 0
5. 0	10. 0	15. +	20. 0

SHORT ANSWER:
1. Tex content on farm, Mason needs to get away.
2. Tex concerned when Mace is sick, Mace caring when Tex is hurt.
3. Typical adolescent friendship confused by awakening sexual instincts.
4. Young image of Tex's own youth.
5. Shot in drug raid, taken by Collins to the hospital. He learns true meaning of his family relationships.

CHALLENGE:

Tex—constructive, reaching and growing. Mace—desire to succeed. Lem Peters moves further into the destructive world of drugs.

ANSWER KEYS (continued)

The Metamorphosis by Franz Kafka

OBJECTIVE:

1. a clerk
2. he will lose his job
3. getting out of bed, opening the door
4. chief clerk
5. taking the key in his teeth
6. his father
7. hitting him with a stick
8. his sister
9. his father went bankrupt
10. furniture is gone
11. loss of sight
12. crawling up the ceiling
13. takes lodgers
14. sights and sounds through the door
15. throwing apples
16. charwoman
17. sister's violin
18. leave
19. charwoman, like garbage
20. going on a picnic

SHORT ANSWER:

1. Faithful worker, good son, takes care of family.
2. That his job will be taken away, that he will be punished for something.
3. Find him disgusting, keep him inside.
4. Hitting him, throwing apples.
5. Becomes a total insect, lives on garbage, crawls around his room, dried up when he dies.

CHALLENGE:

No reason why this has happened, struggle to explain, no communication, response negative from his family, in death becomes garbage.

A Separate Peace by John Knowles

OBJECTIVE:

1. Devon, fifteen years
2. talk his way out of everything
3. war, liberty
4. jumping out of the tree
5. Blitzball
6. the old men
7. at the beach
8. his chances to be the top student
9. Gene bounced the limb
10. walk, play sports
11. Gene deliberately injured him
12. get rid of his guilt
13. Brinker Hadley
14. train for the Olympics
15. pick apples, shovel railroad tracks
16. Leper
17. Determine the cause of the accident
18. Leper
19. Bone marrow goes to his bloodstream
20. He couldn't be part of it

SHORT ANSWER:

1. Buildings more worn, tree seems smaller.
2. Phineas the extrovert, Gene the serious student.
3. Becoming an athlete in Phineas' place.
4. Joins the army. Can't handle the mental reality.
5. Pretending they do not exist.

CHALLENGE:

The ways that Gene deals with his fears about death in coming to terms with the death of Phineas.

ANSWER KEYS (continued)

Christy by Catherine Marshall

OBJECTIVE:

1. M	6. H	11. F	16. P
2. B	7. O	12. R	17. N
3. T	8. J	13. C	18. L
4. K	9. D	14. S	19. I
5. A	10. Q	15. E	20. G

SHORT ANSWER:

1. Wanted to do something good for others.
2. Few books, no equipment, terrible hygienic conditions, suspicion from the people.
3. Superstitious practices, primitive medicine, ancient feuds between families.
4. Religion of love rather than God of anger.
5. Cove people didn't see him as a real man, he was unsure of his own faith.

CHALLENGE:

Growing to love the children, Miss Alice, relationship with Fairlight, Dr. MacNeill, finding her own real faith.

The Heart is a Lonely Hunter by Carson McCullers

OBJECTIVE:

1. 0	6. 0	11. +	16. 0
2. +	7. 0	12. +	17. 0
3. 0	8. +	13. 0	18. +
4. +	9. +	14. +	19. 0
5. 0	10. 0	15. 0	20. 0

SHORT ANSWER:

1. World of reality—world of imagination.
2. Because Singer was such a good listener.
3. By raising the blacks' standard of living and health.
4. Becomes more outgoing, redecorates, relates to people.
5. Job of her own, away from family, dressing up.

CHALLENGE:

Each of these four seeks to find himself. Singer helps as each expresses feelings. Irony that Singer cannot respond. Mick, Biff, Blount, and Dr. Copeland each talk about what is important to him.

The Member of the Wedding by Carson McCullers

OBJECTIVE:

1. B	6. B	11. A	16. A
2. C	7. C	12. C	17. C
3. D	8. C	13. B	18. A
4. C	9. D	14. B	19. C
5. D	10. B	15. D	20. C

ANSWER KEYS (continued)

The Member of the Wedding by Carson McCullers (continued)

SHORT ANSWER:
1. She depends on them for her identity.
2. Wanting to join the club next door, desire to go away with Janice and Jarvis.
3. Listens to them, feeds them, really cares.
4. T.T. just someone to go out with. Ludie was the great love of her life.
5. Neither really belongs anywhere.

CHALLENGE:
Frankie's fantasies at the end of the play are the same as at the beginning. Go around the world with Mary. No growth or grasp of reality.

The Chosen by Chaim Potok

OBJECTIVE:

1. R	6. T	11. S	16. N
2. A	7. L	12. G	17. E
3. I	8. F	13. H	18. C
4. O	9. B	14. P	19. M
5. J	10. K	15. D	20. Q

SHORT ANSWER:
1. Danny hits Reuven with a baseball, later comes to the hospital. Reuven's father suggests that they be friends.
2. Reuven and his father very close, Danny brought up in silence.
3. Brilliant mind, desire to study psychology, not to lead small religious group.
4. Saunders—a religious state, Malter—a political state.
5. To teach Danny to look into his own heart.

CHALLENGE:
Danny will learn to help those who hurt because of the things he has learned about himself.

The Catcher in the Rye by J.D. Salinger

OBJECTIVE:

1. F	6. I	11. D	16. B
2. L	7. G	12. J	17. H
3. T	8. A	13. S	18. K
4. E	9. Q	14. C	19. N
5. R	10. O	15. M	20. P

SHORT ANSWER:
1. Totally refuses to conform to the system.
2. Sally makes him feel like a he-man, Jane he really cared about.
3. Writes about the baseball mitt, keeps dreaming about Allie.
4. He can say to her what he really feels.
5. He can stay in a child's world so he does not have to face reality.

CHALLENGE:
Hides his hurt behind "phoniness", attempt of the typical young man to grow up. Holden can still only relate to children.

ANSWER KEYS (continued)

Shane by Jack Schaefer

OBJECTIVE:

1. B	6. B	11. K	16. G
2. E	7. J	12. H	17. F
3. A	8. C	13. B	18. D
4. G	9. L	14. J	19. C
5. H	10. I	15. A	20. J

SHORT ANSWER:

1. Likes the peaceful farm life—Starrett needs him.
2. Doesn't wear a gun, refuses to talk about himself.
3. Must be used wisely by the man who wears it.
4. By making him realize that they cannot run.
5. Shot Wilson in the bar, Fletcher from the balcony.

CHALLENGE:

Reporter would recount action, interview those who saw the fight, describe Shane's departure.

The Odd Couple by Neil Simon

OBJECTIVE:

1. Felix is late	6. move in	11. is late	16. messes up the house
2. a sportswriter	7. fancy sandwiches	12. gets burned up	17. things Felix does to annoy him
3. a mess	8. they are free	13. telling his troubles	18. get out
4. a telegram	9. watching television	14. to come for dinner	19. feel guilty
5. self-pity	10. in the elevator	15. to go to the girls	20. moves in with the girls

SHORT ANSWER:

1. Has not shown up, has tried to kill himself.
2. Oscar—gruff and messy, Felix—neat and sensitive.
3. Act I a total mess, Act II super-neat and efficient.
4. Air freshener, constant cleaning, fancy dinners, coasters on tables.
5. Felix appeals to their emotions.

CHALLENGE:

Felix doesn't really change. He gets his way by being himself. Oscar becomes more aware of his feelings, especially with his family.

Rabbit, Run by John Updike

OBJECTIVE:

1. B	6. B	11. B	16. B
2. D	7. D	12. B	17. A
3. C	8. A	13. B	18. B
4. D	9. C	14. D	19. B
5. C	10. C	15. C	20. A

ANSWER KEYS (continued)

Rabbit, Run by John Updike (continued)

SHORT ANSWER:

1. From his basketball days. He can never stay and face responsibility.
2. To face his obligations as a family man.
3. Back to his high-school days—the only time that had meaning.
4. Shut in by the routine of family responsibility.
5. Rabbit leaves, Janice gets drunk and drowns the baby.

CHALLENGE:

Same weaknesses of character. Runs away at the beginning, from Ruth when she is pregnant, from Janice a second time. He even runs away from the cemetery.

Macho by Edmund Villasenor

OBJECTIVE:

1. +	6. +	11. +	16. 0
2. 0	7. 0	12. 0	17. +
3. 0	8. 0	13. +	18. 0
4. +	9. 0	14. 0	19. 0
5. 0	10. +	15. +	20. 0

SHORT ANSWER:

1. Father a drunk who doesn't work—no money to take care of younger children.
2. Took money for fake papers, food at high prices, men killed in illegal entry attempts.
3. He became the father Roberto did not have, Roberto was his substitute son.
4. Must revenge the insult, code of honor before love.
5. Revenge before love.

CHALLENGE:

Work responsibility on the ranch, trip north to learn the realities of life, love for Lydia, return home to responsibilities.

Unit 2
Steps Back in Time

Synopses

Elizabeth the Queen
by Maxwell Anderson

Set in the court of Elizabeth I of England, this powerful historical drama presents the queen and the woman as Elizabeth is forced to choose between the man she loves, Lord Essex, and her throne. Through a plot engineered by Essex's political enemies, the ambitious noble is separated from Elizabeth and sent on a hopeless military mission to Ireland. Messages between Essex and Elizabeth never reach their intended destination. When Essex returns home, his rebellious troops seize the palace. Because Essex desires the throne, Elizabeth is forced to arrest him for treason. Until the last moment she hopes her proud lover will ask for mercy. The confrontation scenes between Elizabeth and Essex present a very human view of history. The woman who must be first the queen is left alone.

Becket
by Jean Anouilh

In eleventh-century England, King Henry II sows his wild oats with his Saxon friend, Thomas Becket. Becket tries to teach the young monarch how to be a ruler. In an attempt to break the power of the Church of England, Henry appoints Becket as Archbishop of Canterbury. The king mistakenly believes that Becket will become his tool. The new archbishop, however, has found a new purpose for his life. As Becket honors his vows to God, he becomes Henry's mortal enemy. The love-hate relationship between the two men remains until Becket is assassinated. The archbishop wins in death as the king must acknowledge the power of the Church within his realm. Yet, Henry the man still loves the friend he has lost.

A Tale of Two Cities
by Charles Dickens

This epic novel tells the story of people caught in the political and social turmoil of the French Revolution. Lucie Manette and her father, a former political prisoner in the hated Bastille, return to England to build a new life. Lucie's love for Charles Darnay is endangered because Charles is a member of the hated Evremonde family, the most ruthless branch of the French aristocracy. When the Revolution explodes in 1779, Charles is drawn back to Paris in an effort to save a faithful family servant. Charles and Lucie's lives are endangered by the vicious Madame DeFarge and the bloodthirsty mobs of Paris. Only Sidney Carton, a drunken wastrel who has loved Lucie from afar, can save Charles from certain death. Dickens' well-constructed plot and superb characters show the ways in which the larger currents of history can affect the lives of ordinary people.

April Morning
by Howard Fast

The maturation of Adam Cooper of Lexington, Massachusetts takes place in one day, April 18, 1775. When the men of the Lexington militia learn that the British are marching from Boston to seize stores of ammunition, the farmers muster to defend their homes. Adam has never felt close to his father Moses; yet love between father and son is expressed for the first time just before Moses becomes one of the first casualties of the American Revolution. Adam sees first-hand the realities of death, for both American and British soldiers alike. After his father's death, Adam must become the head of his family. He knows that the fighting must continue in order to drive the British out altogether. During the several skirmishes in which he participates in one day of combat, Adam becomes a young man who can face his new responsibilities. This novel is written very simply; however, the war becomes very real when it is seen through one boy's eyes.

Cimarron
by Edna Ferber

Yancey and Sabra Cravat come to the Oklahoma Territory during the wild land rush of the 1880s. As the years pass, the family builds a life in Osage, the small settlement that becomes a boom town. Yancey becomes a legend through his flashy dress and daring exploits. Sabra is the guiding force behind *The Wigwam*, the local newspaper. The discovery of oil in the territory changes life forever. The citizens gain more wealth than they know how to use. Yancey disappears for weeks at a time on various quixotic adventures. Sabra becomes increasingly involved in local and state politics. Frontier men have been pictured in many novels as strong, colorful figures. This narrative shows Edna Ferber's strong belief that the strength of the pioneer woman was largely responsible for the building of the American West.

The Great Gatsby
by F. Scott Fitzgerald

At the height of the Roaring Twenties, Nick Carroway, an average young man from the Midwest, comes to Long Island and moves in next door to the wealthy and mysterious Jay Gatsby. Nick becomes involved in Gatsby's swinging lifestyle. Nick learns of Gatsby's idealized love for Daisy, the wife of Tom Buchanan. Nick assists Gatsby in arranging meetings with Daisy. Contrasted with Gatsby's and Daisy's love is Tom's rather sordid relationship with Myrtle Wilson. When Myrtle is accidently killed, her enraged husband believes that Gatsby is responsible. The final scenes of the novel show the emptiness of wealth as Gatsby's body floats face down in his swimming pool. The vision of life as a grand party is gone forever. This novel presents the same "jazz age" lifestyle which destroyed Scott and Zelda Fitzgerald. The quest for pleasure ends in nothingness when the bottom falls out.

Johnny Tremain
by Esther Forbes

Johnny Tremain is a promising young silversmith living in Boston just before the American Revolution. An accident injures Johnny's hand, ends his usefulness at the Laphams, and destroys his hopes for a career as a craftsman. After a period of wandering and bitterness, Johnny meets Rab, a young printer, and becomes involved in the exciting activities of the Sons of Liberty. Johnny also must solve a very personal mystery. His dead mother had left him a cup bearing the family crest of Mr. Lyte, a wealthy Boston merchant. When Johnny tries to establish a connection with the Lyte family, he is accused of theft. Johnny is also angered and fascinated by the beautiful Lavinia Lyte, the belle of Boston. This novel presents both the British and the Americans as men caught in the current of the times. As war with England becomes inevitable, Johnny becomes a rider and a courier. His friend Rab obtains a musket from a very ordinary British soldier, who is later shot for desertion. The climax of the novel comes in the exciting account of the Boston Tea Party. This fine historical novel presents one young man's growth and the birth of a new nation.

The Lion in Winter
by William Goldman

Aging King Henry II will soon be forced to choose an heir to his kingdom. Who will win the fight for political power? Will it be Richard, Geoffrey, or John? Henry knows that the real threat to his power is his wife, Eleanor of Aquitaine. The play takes place at Christmastime, when the queen has been released from prison to attend Christmas Court at Chinon Castle. The king and queen verbally spar with each other, taunt each other, and plot against one another. The prize is the crown of England. In spite of this feud, Henry and Eleanor still love each other because they are perfectly matched antagonists. This play presents, in the vitality of his old age, the same king who is portrayed as a young man in *Becket*.

The House of the Seven Gables
by Nathaniel Hawthorne

Set in Salem, Massachusetts in the nineteenth century, this novel shows the psychological consequences that the sins of one generation can have on the next. The Pyncheons, owners of the House of the Seven Gables, bear the curse of Matthew Maule, who was hanged so that the first Pyncheon might steal his land to build the mansion. Hepzibah Pyncheon, a withered old maid, lives in the musty house awaiting the return of her brother Clifford. Phoebe, a young country cousin, comes to share Hepzibah's home and to brighten her life. Phoebe also falls in love with Holgrave, a young artist. When Clifford returns, he and his sister try to free themselves from the threats of the present Judge Pyncheon and from the ghosts of the past. Phoebe and Holgrave also must fight the shadows of the past to secure their love. Hawthorne has presented a powerful study in the psychology of guilt and its consequences.

The Scarlet Letter
by Nathaniel Hawthorne

The Scarlet Letter is a powerful psychological novel which reveals the destructive consequences of hidden guilt. Hester Prynne, the novel's heroine, has been found guilty of adultery. Her husband, Roger Chillingworth, is determined to learn the identity of Hester's lover. The town's Puritan minister, Arthur Dimmesdale, struggles with the torments of his own soul. The novel chronicles seven years in the lives of these three. Hester faces the community alone, finding strength for survival as she cares for her child. Dimmesdale progressively deteriorates because his guilt is hidden. Chillingworth becomes a demon in human form as he relentlessly seeks revenge. *The Scarlet Letter* presents a clear study of the interior world of these characters, played against the backdrop of harsh Puritan Boston. The narrative provides a fascinating study in the depths of human personality.

The Country of the Pointed Firs
by Sarah Orne Jewett

In the mid-1850s, a young writer from the city goes to spend the summer in Dunnet Landing, a small community on the coast of Maine. Her landlady, Mrs. Almira Todd, is an herb specialist and a narrator of the community's history. The book is a collection of short narratives linked by the accounts of the young writer's encounters with the various inhabitants of Dunnet Landing. She hears the tales of Elijah Tilley, of the forsaken recluse Joanna, and of Almira's own love Nathan, who was lost at sea. The city girl also meets characters who impart local color as she visits Almira's mother, attends the Blackett family reunion, and visits with a woman who believes herself to be the twin of Queen Victoria. This fine narrative collection is a beautiful picture of life in seafaring New England during the late nineteenth century.

Dr. Zhivago
by Boris Pasternak

Against the massive background of the Russian Revolution of 1917, the reader sees the life of one man, physician Yuri Zhivago. Young Zhivago marries Tonia, the daughter of an aristocratic family. After he sends his family to the country for safety, Yuri meets the beautiful Lara. Lara, victimized as a child by the brutal Komarovsky, has married Pasha, the young idealist who eventually becomes a general of the Revolution. After a brief affair with Lara, Yuri decides that he must return to his family. The young doctor is, however, kidnapped by one of the warring revolutionary groups. Yuri experiences war in its most brutal forms. After the doctor escapes from his captors, he and Lara meet again and spend a brief time in the country village of Varykino. The two lovers live an idyllic existence in the midst of a world at war. As the wolves surround their villa, the lovers must part. This novel is a masterpiece of historical fiction, in which Nobel prize winner Pasternak shows how individuals must struggle for their humanity. Hope lies in being able to snatch a moment of love before the final separation comes.

The Winthrop Woman
by Anya Seton

This novel portrays the lives of the determined Puritans who settled New England in the 1630s. Elizabeth Winthrop, niece of Massachusetts Bay leader John Winthrop, loves John's son Jack, but is married to Harry Winthrop instead. After Harry is killed, Elizabeth immigrates with the Winthrop party to Massachusetts. Married to weak Robert Feake, Elizabeth becomes the steadying force in her family and exerts the strength of her personality. She defies the autocratic rule of her uncle John. Her support of religious heretic Anne Hutchinson and her defiance of authority cause Elizabeth to be accused of witchcraft and to be driven out of Massachusetts Bay. Elizabeth and her husband are assisted in their flight to Connecticut by sea captain Thomas Hallet. Elizabeth and Hallet fall in love. After Feake becomes totally unstable, Elizabeth seeks a civil divorce in the Dutch colony of New Amsterdam so she and Hallet can be married. *The Winthrop Woman* might be well compared with *Cimarron* (p. 52). Like Sabra Cravat, Elizabeth is a survivor. She builds a new life in a new land by the sheer force of her will and by the defiance of arbitrary authority. This novel is an excellent picture of the realities of daily life in colonial America.

Exodus
by Leon Uris

This novel of the Jewish settlement of Palestine and the establishment of the state of Israel shows determined men and women who survived the pogroms of Russia and the holocaust of Germany to build a homeland for their people. The personal histories of freedom fighters Ari and Barak Ben Canaan and Dov Landau are told in flashbacks. The main plot of the novel is a story of great courage. American nurse Kitty Fremont and German refugee Karen Hansen work with the freedom fighters. They defeat the British blockade of Palestine by running a shipload of refugee children from Cyprus to Tel Aviv. The novel contains several beautiful love stories: Barak and Sarah, Ari and Kitty, Dov and Karen. Human tenderness must be found in moments surrounded by violence and terrorism. Leon Uris gives the reader a strong sense of the past, present, and future of the Jewish people.

The Friendly Persuasion
by Jessamyn West

Jess Birdwell is a Quaker nurseryman in Pennsylvania in the 1830s–1850s. His wife Eliza is a Quaker minister. Despite their differences of temperament, Jess and Eliza love each other deeply. That love survives the loss of a child as well as many lesser family tribulations. The book's loosely-woven plot recounts various episodes in the lives of various family members. The children, Josh, young Jess, and Mattie, all gain a strength and determination inherited from their parents. Some episodes are very light in tone: the story of Samantha, the pacing goose, and Jess's purchase of Lady, a most unlikely race horse. Other episodes deal with more serious choices. Josh must choose between his family's nonviolent religious beliefs and his need to defend his family as the Civil War approaches. The novel's characters are each complete short stories which reaffirm the enormous value to be found in the lives of ordinary people.

The Caine Mutiny Court-Martial
by Herman Wouk

This dramatic adaptation of Wouk's novel considers how leaders are responsible for behaving during times of pressure in combat. Maryk, the executive officer of the minesweeper *Caine*, is being court-martialed for leading a mutiny. The defense contends that Captain Queeg was too mentally unstable to retain his command, and that Maryk acted to save the ship. The officers of the court must decide if this action was mutiny. Lieutenant Keefer, a novelist and amateur psychologist, wished to get even with Queeg. Keefer fed Maryk the information necessary to make the executive officer believe that the captain was unbalanced. Greenwald, the counsel for the defense, must prove that Queeg is mentally incompetent. The tension in the courtroom mounts as the captain is called as the chief defense witness. How much discipline was necessary on the ship? Was Queeg acting in the best interests of his crew? Were his harsh acts simply good military discipline? This play probes many aspects of the effects of wars on the men who fight them.

Name _____ Date _____

Elizabeth the Queen by Maxwell Anderson

Correctly complete each sentence with information from the novel.

1. The lady-in-waiting who also loves Essex is _____.

2. At court, Essex's most dangerous enemies are _____ and _____.

3. Essex angers Raleigh by making fun of _____.

4. A great military victory had been won by Essex at _____.

5. In council, Essex urges Elizabeth to _____.

6. Essex's closest friend at court is _____.

7. Raleigh tricks Essex into leading an army into _____.

8. Essex's greatest weakness is his _____.

9. Elizabeth is forced to choose between _____ and _____.

10. For his protection against her own anger, the queen gives Essex _____.

11. The queen does not receive Essex's letters because _____.

12. Upon his return to England, Essex refuses to _____.

13. A messenger tells Elizabeth that _____.

14. Essex most wants to be _____.

15. After Essex dismisses his troops, Elizabeth _____.

16. Before Essex's execution, the queen waits for _____.

17. To distract the queen, the actors present a scene from _____.

18. When Essex comes, Elizabeth offers to _____.

19. Essex says that the only thing in life he regrets leaving is _____.

20. At the end of the play, the queen is left alone with _____.

Great Books for Independent Reading

Name _____ Date _____

Elizabeth the Queen by Maxwell Anderson

Answer each of the following questions in two or three complete sentences.

1. In the opening scene, what schemes are being plotted by the two court factions?

    _____

    _____

    _____

    _____

2. How is Essex tricked into going to Ireland?

    _____

    _____

    _____

    _____

3. How does the queen show the disturbed state of mind that her love for Essex has created?

    _____

    _____

    _____

    _____

4. How does the play show the popularity of Essex with the common people? Why does Elizabeth fear this popularity?

    _____

    _____

    _____

    _____

5. Why does Essex refuse to allow the queen to spare his life?

    _____

    _____

    _____

    _____

Challenge

Write an essay describing the internal conflict of the play between Elizabeth the Queen and Elizabeth the woman. At the end, what does Elizabeth win and what does she lose?

Name _____   Date _____

Becket by Jean Anouilh

In the numbered blanks at the left, write the letter of the matching person, place, or thing.

_____ 1. Becket's servant and friend

_____ 2. Saxon who collaborated with the Normans

_____ 3. Torn between a need for love and a desire for power

_____ 4. Rose up to protect Becket when he returned to England

_____ 5. Home of the young Saxon monk

_____ 6. First office given to Becket

_____ 7. Bishop of London, Becket's enemy

_____ 8. Hated Becket as "competition" for Henry's love

_____ 9. Becket's Welch mistress

_____ 10. Where Becket took refuge in France

_____ 11. Showed great humanity and understanding for the Saxon common people

_____ 12. Given by Henry in exchange for Gwendolen

_____ 13. Flogged Henry

_____ 14. Had been Becket's spiritual father

_____ 15. Took money from Henry and helped Becket at the same time

_____ 16. Was to be crowned before his father's death

_____ 17. Banishing a person from the rites of the Church

_____ 18. Negotiated the final meeting between Henry and Becket

_____ 19. Becket's killers

_____ 20. Scene of Becket's death

A. Becket's father
B. Hastings
C. Archbishop of Canterbury
D. Gwendolen
E. Folliot
F. Henry III
G. Becket
H. Louis of France
I. Chancellor
J. Young Monk
K. Abbey of St. Martin
L. Canterbury Cathedral
M. The Queen
N. Excommunication
O. Saxon common people
P. Norman barons
Q. Saxon peasant girl
R. The Pope
S. Saxon monks
T. Henry

Name _____   Date _____

Becket by Jean Anouilh

Answer each of the following questions in two or three complete sentences.

1. In the scene with the Saxon peasant family, how does Becket show that he is more humane than Henry is?

    _____
    _____
    _____
    _____

2. Why does Becket spare the life of the young Saxon monk?

    _____
    _____
    _____
    _____

3. How does Becket change after he becomes Archbishop of Canterbury?

    _____
    _____
    _____
    _____

4. Why does Becket decide to come out of hiding and return to his post as Archbishop?

    _____
    _____
    _____
    _____

5. How does the final meeting scene show Henry's loneliness and confusion?

    _____
    _____
    _____
    _____

Challenge

A developing character is one who changes by growth and experience. Write an essay to explain which of the two is the more developing character, Henry or Becket. Support your answer with evidence from the play.

Great Books for Independent Reading

Name _____   Date _____

A Tale of Two Cities by Charles Dickens

In the numbered blanks at the left, write the letter of the matching person or place. You may use a letter more than once.

_____	1.	The most hated aristocratic name in France
_____	2.	London residence of the Manettes
_____	3.	Loyal employee of Tellson's bank
_____	4.	French hometown of Dr. Manette
_____	5.	The Golden Thread
_____	6.	Worked as a spy on both sides of the Revolution
_____	7.	Was acquitted on a charge of treason against the King of England
_____	8.	Secret society of the French Revolution
_____	9.	Prisoner in 105 North Tower
_____	10.	Faithful servant who cared for his former employer
_____	11.	Poorest section of Paris
_____	12.	Had been responsible for the death of Madame DeFarge's family
_____	13.	Gave his life to save the life of another
_____	14.	Was fiercely protective of her "Lady Bird"
_____	15.	Gained his legal reputation through the hard work of another
_____	16.	Kept the records of those who would be exterminated by the Revolution
_____	17.	Symbol of French oppression and injustice
_____	18.	Was hanged for the murder of an aristocrat
_____	19.	Described himself as a "fisherman"
_____	20.	Wrote to his former employer for help

A. Jarvis Lorry
B. Alexandre Manette
C. Miss Pross
D. Lucie Manette
E. Jerry Cruncher
F. Madame DeFarge
G. Gabelle
H. John Basard
I. Monsieur DeFarge
J. Evremonde
K. Monsieur Le Marquis
L. Mr. Stryver
M. Charles Darnay
N. Saint Antoine
O. Beauvais
P. Bastille
Q. Sidney Carton
R. Soho
S. Jacques

Name _____   Date _____

A Tale of Two Cities by Charles Dickens

Answer each of the following questions in two or three complete sentences.

1.   Why does Mr. Lorry go to meet Miss Manette in Dover?

_____

_____

_____

_____

2.   Why are Stryver and Carton called "the lion and the jackal"?

_____

_____

_____

_____

3.   How does Charles Darnay differ from his uncle in his attitude toward wealth and class privilege?

_____

_____

_____

_____

4.   Why is the term, "a man of business," an ironic contradiction to Jarvis Lorry's real character?

_____

_____

_____

_____

5.   How does Sidney Carton get into LaForce, and how does he get Charles Darnay out?

_____

_____

_____

_____

Challenge

Loyalty and love, even at the cost of great personal sacrifice, are major themes in *A Tale of Two Cities*. Discuss three characters, and the way that each illustrates such loyalty in his/her actions.

©1986, 1991 J. Weston Walch, Publisher

Name _____   Date _____

April Morning by Howard Fast

Correctly complete each sentence with information from the novel.

1. The events of this novel cover a period of _____.

2. Moses Cooper most loved to _____.

3. _____ was Adam's younger brother.

4. Of all his family members, Adam was closest to _____.

5. Adam officially joins the Lexington militia by _____.

6. _____ was the commander of the Lexington militia.

7. Joseph Simmons was a _____ by profession.

8. The militia appointed _____ as their spokesman to talk with the British.

9. The first Lexington man shot by the British was _____.

10. The main highway from Concord to Boston was the _____.

11. _____ found Adam in the woods, and took him to the gathering of the other militiamen.

12. The militia attacked the British army from _____.

13. _____ became a substitute father for Adam and his brother.

14. The militia was divided into two companies: men with _____, and men with _____.

15. The first dead soldier that Adam saw up close was _____.

16. For a time, the men thought Adam was dead because he _____.

17. The Lexington militia helped drive the British back to _____.

18. Adam decided to marry _____.

19. Adam's mother sent him to church with _____.

20. All of the militiamen were planning to muster for _____.

©1986, 1991 J. Weston Walch, Publisher   *Great Books for Independent Reading*

Name _____ Date _____

April Morning by Howard Fast

Answer each of the following questions in two or three complete sentences.

1. Why did Adam think that his father hated him?

    _____

    _____

    _____

    _____

2. On the night before the fighting began, how did Moses Cooper show his love for his son?

    _____

    _____

    _____

    _____

3. What did the Lexington men plan to do when the British came? Why did this plan fail?

    _____

    _____

    _____

    _____

4. Why did Cousin Simmons tell Adam that the fighting must continue?

    _____

    _____

    _____

5. How does Adam Cooper change in a single day?

    _____

    _____

    _____

Challenge

Write an essay describing some of the things that may happen to Adam Cooper in the days and weeks that followed the Battle of Lexington.

©1986, 1991 J. Weston Walch, Publisher

Great Books for Independent Reading

Name _____ Date _____

Cimarron by Edna Ferber

Select the letter of the word or phrase which correctly completes each statement.

_____ 1. Yancey and Sabra came to Oklahoma from (A) Massachusetts (B) Kentucky (C) Mississippi (D) Kansas.

_____ 2. Yancey intended to earn his living by (A) mining (B) selling real estate (C) practicing law (D) publishing a newspaper.

_____ 3. Sabra's most valuable possession brought from her old home was (A) her china (B) Mother Briget's quilt (C) the silver (D) the family photo album.

_____ 4. Yancey did all of the following in Osage except (A) conduct a church service (B) practice law (C) write flaming editorials (D) run for public office.

_____ 5. Of greatest help to Sabra during their first years in Oklahoma was (A) Cim (B) Isaiah (C) Ruby (D) Jesse.

_____ 6. Yancey left Sabra the first time to (A) fight in World War I (B) participate in another land run (C) drill for oil (D) run for Congress.

_____ 7. When Sabra went home to visit, she (A) decided to stay (B) was bored (C) loved the life of luxury again (D) decided to divorce Yancey.

_____ 8. Yancey's most spectacular court appearance was in defense of (A) Dixie Lee (B) Pegler (C) the Kid (D) Sol Levy.

_____ 9. *The Wigwam* was a success through the efforts of (A) Yancey (B) Jesse (C) Sabra (D) the territorial government.

_____ 10. Yancey continually championed the cause of (A) the oil men (B) the original settlers (C) the Indians (D) the ranch owners.

_____ 11. Isaiah was killed by (A) outlaws (B) Indian torture (C) a tornado (D) a white posse.

_____ 12. Sabra gained influence in the community through (A) the paper (B) women's groups (C) political involvement (D) all of the above.

_____ 13. The rich man who always remained an outsider was (A) Sol Levy (B) Tracy Wyatt (C) Big Elk (D) Doctor Valliant.

_____ 14. Donna Cravat (A) was sent to finishing school (B) married a rich man (C) was a great disappointment to her mother (D) all of the above.

_____ 15. The total social revolution in Osage came with the discovery of (A) oil (B) gold (C) silver (D) copper.

_____ 16. Yancey forced Sabra to (A) shut down the paper (B) stay out of politics (C) attend her son's wedding (D) not to hire any more Indian help.

_____ 17. Sabra was elected (A) mayor (B) governor (C) Congresswoman (D) chairman of the town's political action committee.

_____ 18. The statue representing pioneer spirit was a portrait of (A) Sabra (B) Yancey (C) the Kid (D) young Cim.

_____ 19. The symbol of real power behind the growth of Oklahoma, according to Edna Ferber, was (A) the rifle (B) the covered wagon (C) the sunbonnet (D) the oil well.

_____ 20. Yancey Cravat died (A) on an oil field (B) after he had saved the lives of others (C) in the arms of his wife (D) all of the above.

Great Books for Independent Reading

Name _____ Date _____

Cimarron by Edna Ferber

Answer each of the following questions in two or three complete sentences.

1. Describe how Yancey lost his claim when he made his first land run.

    _____
    _____
    _____
    _____

2. What characteristics quickly made Yancey an Oklahoma legend?

    _____
    _____
    _____
    _____

3. How did Sabra keep the family together during Yancey's long absences?

    _____
    _____
    _____
    _____

4. Why were both of Sabra's children a disappointment to her?

    _____
    _____
    _____
    _____

5. How did the discovery of oil drastically change life in Oklahoma?

    _____
    _____
    _____
    _____

Challenge

How were both Sabra and Yancey Cravat symbols of the pioneer spirit which developed the American West?

Great Books for Independent Reading

Name _____ Date _____

The Great Gatsby by F. Scott Fitzgerald

Correctly complete each sentence with information from the novel.

1. The story is told by _____.

2. Nick meets Gatsby when _____.

3. Jordan Baker's boredom with life is shown by _____.

4. Daisy believes the best thing a girl can be in this world is _____

   _____.

5. Four adjectives which would best describe Gatsby's parties are _____ ,

   _____ , _____ , and _____.

6. The area between Long Island and the city is called _____ ,

   and is presided over by _____.

7. Nick sees Gatsby staring across the water at _____.

8. Myrtle Wilson may be totally contrasted with Daisy as _____.

9. The party at Tom's city apartment ends abruptly when _____.

10. When he attends Gatsby's party, the only person Nick knows is _____.

11. Nick learns from Jordan the story of _____.

12. Daisy did not marry Gatsby because _____.

13. The big mystery about Gatsby's money was _____.

14. Nick made arrangements for a meeting between _____

    at _____.

15. When they toured Gatsby's mansion, Daisy is most emotionally affected by _____.

16. Gatsby had inherited his money from _____.

17. When the group goes to the city, Tom drives _____.

18. Myrtle is jealous when she thinks that _____ is _____.

19. Myrtle Wilson is killed by _____ , but _____ takes the blame.

20. Wilson shoots Gatsby because _____.

Great Books for Independent Reading

Name _____ Date _____

The Great Gatsby by F. Scott Fitzgerald

Answer each of the following questions in two or three complete sentences.

1. Nick says that Tom and Daisy were "careless people." How does the novel support this statement?

    _____

    _____

    _____

    _____

2. Why does Nick, as an outside observer, make an effective narrator?

    _____

    _____

    _____

    _____

3. How is the reality of Gatsby's past contrasted to the false image of wealth that he has presented to the world?

    _____

    _____

    _____

    _____

4. How do Tom and Gatsby present a definite study in contrast?

    _____

    _____

    _____

    _____

5. How is Gatsby's funeral scene a contrast to the party scenes presented earlier in the novel?

    _____

    _____

    _____

    _____

Challenge

Write an essay citing specific scenes from *The Great Gatsby* which illustrate the lostness of the American fun-seeking generation of the 1920s.

©1986, 1991 J. Weston Walch, Publisher

Name _____ Date _____

Johnny Tremain by Esther Forbes

Select the letter of the word or phrase which correctly completes each statement.

_____ 1. Johnny had been apprenticed to Mr. Lapham at the request of (A) his father (B) Paul Revere (C) his mother (D) Mrs. Lapham.

_____ 2. Johnny bossed the other apprentices because (A) he was older (B) he was more skilled as a silversmith (C) he was bigger (D) he was related to the Laphams.

_____ 3. Johnny injured his hand while he was making a sugar bowl for (A) Lavinia Lyte (B) John Hancock (C) James Otis (D) Paul Revere.

_____ 4. Mrs. Lapham did not call a doctor when Johnny injured his hand because (A) she didn't care about Johnny (B) working on the Sabbath was illegal (C) she didn't want Mr. Lapham to know that they had been working (D) she didn't want Dove to get into any trouble.

_____ 5. Of all the Lapham girls, Johnny was closest to (A) Madge (B) Dorcas (C) Isannah (D) Cilla.

_____ 6. After he was injured, the first job that Johnny could get was (A) with a butcher (B) with Mr. Hancock (C) with the *Observer* (D) at the Lytes.

_____ 7. The Observers were (A) a secret political organization (B) a group of British sympathizers (C) a social club (D) a branch of the colonial militia.

_____ 8. The British officer who became Johnny's friend was (A) Lt. Stranger (B) Col. Smith (C) Sgt. Gale (D) Maj. Pitcairn.

_____ 9. Mr. Tweedie was finally married to (A) Madge (B) Dorcas (C) Mrs. Lapham (D) Cilla.

_____ 10. Johnny's sources of information about British activities included (A) Dove (B) wastebasket scraps (C) Lydia (D) all of the above.

_____ 11. Rab finally got his musket (A) from Sgt. Gale (B) from Pumpkin (C) by stealing it (D) from the stable at the Afric Queen.

_____ 12. Uncle Lorne's contribution to the rebellion was as a (A) printer (B) spy (C) rider and courier (D) gunsmith.

_____ 13. The greatest orator in Boston was (A) Sam Adams (B) Paul Revere (C) James Otis (D) Dr. Warren.

_____ 14. Johnny learned the truth of his relationship with the Lyte family from (A) Lavinia (B) the judge in court (C) Mr. Lyte (D) Bessie the housekeeper.

_____ 15. Johnny got out of Boston by (A) riding Goblin (B) pretending to be drunk (C) disguising himself as a British private (D) stowing away on a ship.

_____ 16. The one who died of wounds received at Lexington was (A) Rab (B) Pumpkin (C) Dr. Warren (D) Grandsire Silsbee.

_____ 17. Isannah Lapham (A) died of illness (B) went to England with Lavinia (C) went home to live with her mother (D) married Johnny.

_____ 18. The British soldiers in this novel are presented as (A) totally evil men (B) enemies of all colonials (C) ordinary men with a nasty job to do (D) men without thoughts or personalities.

_____ 19. Johnny's attitude most greatly changes toward (A) Dove (B) Cilla (C) Rab (D) Mr. Lyte.

_____ 20. Dr. Warren says that he can operate on Johnny's hand so Johnny will be able to (A) fire a gun (B) become a silversmith (C) work in a print shop (D) make bullets.

Great Books for Independent Reading

Name _____ Date _____

Johnny Tremain by Esther Forbes

Answer each of the following questions in two or three complete sentences.

1. How does Johnny injure his hand?

   _____

   _____

   _____

   _____

2. How does Johnny change after he is injured?

   _____

   _____

   _____

   _____

3. In what ways does Johnny become useful to the Sons of Liberty?

   _____

   _____

   _____

   _____

4. What are Johnny's connections with the Lyte family?

   _____

   _____

   _____

   _____

5. What does James Otis mean when he says that the colonials must fight "so that a man can stand up"?

   _____

   _____

   _____

   _____

Challenge

What are some of the ways that Esther Forbes presents both the British and the Americans as people who are caught up in forces of conflict which are beyond their control?

Great Books for Independent Reading

Name _____   Date _____

The Lion in Winter by James Goldman

In the numbered blanks at the left, write the letter of the matching person or place. You may use a letter more than once.

_____ 1. Henry's eldest son who had died

_____ 2. Determined to leave his kingdom intact to only one of his sons

_____ 3. Had raised Alais as a child

_____ 4. Refused to be called any man's "boy"

_____ 5. Philip's sister, who had been promised in marriage to Richard

_____ 6. Sought Philip as an ally in a war against his father

_____ 7. Middle son with the cold, calculating mind

_____ 8. Section of France that had been Eleanor's dowry

_____ 9. Youngest, weakest, most disgusting of Henry's sons

_____ 10. Could resist almost any temptation except Henry's offer of freedom

_____ 11. Time when the main action of the play takes place

_____ 12. Setting of the play

_____ 13. Henry's friend and personal messenger

_____ 14. Eleanor's favorite son

_____ 15. Where Eleanor was imprisoned

_____ 16. Eleanor's first husband

_____ 17. Son not mentioned as a possible king

_____ 18. Wanted a divorce so he could marry and have more sons

_____ 19. Henry's mistress whom Eleanor hated

_____ 20. Land that was Alais' dowry

A. Alais Capet
B. Chinon Castle
C. Salisbury Tower
D. Prince Henry
E. Richard
F. John
G. Rosamund
H. Henry II
I. Eleanor
J. Geoffrey
K. Christmas Court
L. William Marshal
M. Aquitaine
N. Philip of France
O. Louis of France
P. Vixen

Name _____ Date _____

The Lion in Winter by James Goldman

Answer each of the following questions in two or three complete sentences.

1. How does the play show that Eleanor and Henry enjoy the plots that they are constantly hatching against each other?

    _____

    _____

    _____

    _____

2. How is Alais a victim of the plots of the other characters?

    _____

    _____

    _____

    _____

3. Why does Geoffrey feel neglected and angry?

    _____

    _____

    _____

    _____

4. What does Eleanor finally admit is the one thing that she really wants?

    _____

    _____

    _____

    _____

5. How does the audience know, at the end of the play, that this family feud is not over?

    _____

    _____

    _____

    _____

Challenge

Write an essay to defend or refute the following statement: Despite their many feuds, Henry II and his Queen Eleanor still love each other deeply.

Great Books for Independent Reading

Name _____ Date _____

The House of the Seven Gables by Nathaniel Hawthorne

Select the letter of the word or phrase which correctly completes each statement.

_____ 1. The House of the Seven Gables had been built by (A) Colonel Pyncheon (B) Clifford (C) Matthew Maule (D) Cousin Jaffrey.

_____ 2. In order to seize the land that he desired, Pyncheon had Matthew Maule (A) executed as a wizard (B) run out of town (C) financially ruined (D) thrown into prison.

_____ 3. The people of the town believed that the house was (A) elegant (B) well-built (C) cursed (D) all of the above.

_____ 4. On the day that the house was to have had its first great reception, the Colonel (A) died (B) became governor (C) established his land claim (D) married his new bride.

_____ 5. Hepzibah may be described as (A) homely (B) shy (C) loyal (D) all of the above.

_____ 6. Jaffrey Pyncheon (A) genuinely wants to help Hepzibah (B) dislikes Phoebe (C) looks just like the Colonel (D) is very fond of Clifford.

_____ 7. Hepzibah's closest friend and helper becomes (A) Holgrave (B) Phoebe (C) Cousin Alice (D) Uncle Venner.

_____ 8. Phoebe (A) takes over the shopkeeping chores (B) helps Clifford (C) is a good gardener (D) all of the above.

_____ 9. After his return to the house, Clifford is (A) aggressive and violent (B) childlike (C) a total recluse (D) determined to get revenge.

_____ 10. When Jaffrey wants to see Clifford, Hepzibah (A) faints (B) absolutely refuses (C) begs Jaffrey to leave (D) calls the police.

_____ 11. Holgrave the daguerreotypist (A) has been to Europe (B) has practiced hypnosis (C) writes short stories (D) all of the above.

_____ 12. Alice Pyncheon was destroyed by (A) her father's greed (B) her own poor health (C) Maule's desire for revenge (D) her weak mind.

_____ 13. Uncle Venner may be described as (A) an optimist (B) the town philosopher (C) an eccentric (D) all of the above.

_____ 14. Phoebe has to return home (A) because her mother is ill (B) to finish taking care of some personal matters (C) because she is afraid of Clifford (D) because Jaffrey tells her to leave.

_____ 15. Jaffrey wants Clifford to surrender (A) the combination to the safe (B) the deed to the house (C) the documents regarding the missing land claim (D) the personal letters of Judge Pyncheon.

_____ 16. Jaffrey threatens to send Clifford (A) to an insane asylum (B) back to prison (C) to the hospital (D) out of the country.

_____ 17. Jaffrey Pyncheon dies (A) when Hepzibah shoots him (B) when Clifford strangles him (C) in the same way the Colonel had died (D) of food poisoning.

_____ 18. When they find Jaffrey's body, Clifford and Hepzibah (A) run away (B) notify the constable (C) turn to Holgrave for help (D) hide the body in a closet.

_____ 19. Holgrave views Pyncheon's death as (A) part of the curse (B) a fulfillment of Maule's prophecy (C) a just punishment for Jaffrey's wickedness (D) all of the above.

_____ 20. At end of the novel, the House of the Seven Gables (A) falls into ruin (B) is owned by Phoebe and Holgrave (C) is cared for by Uncle Venner (D) burns down.

Name _____ Date _____

The House of the Seven Gables by Nathaniel Hawthorne

Answer each of the following questions in two or three complete sentences.

1. How is Hepzibah exactly like the house itself?

   _____

   _____

   _____

   _____

2. Tell briefly why the house is supposed to have been cursed.

   _____

   _____

   _____

   _____

3. How does Phoebe's arrival change the lives of Hepzibah and Clifford?

   _____

   _____

   _____

   _____

4. Why did Jaffrey have Clifford sent to prison?

   _____

   _____

   _____

   _____

5. Why are Uncle Venner and Holgrave important characters in the story?

   _____

   _____

   _____

   _____

Challenge

One of Nathaniel Hawthorne's major literary themes is that sin and guilt in one generation greatly affect all future generations. Explain how this theme is illustrated in *The House of the Seven Gables.*

Great Books for Independent Reading

Name _____   Date _____

The Scarlet Letter by Nathaniel Hawthorne

Select the letter of the word or phrase which correctly completes each statement.

_____ 1. The setting of the novel is (A) London (B) Virginia (C) Massachusetts (D) New York.

_____ 2. For her crime of adultery, Hester is sentenced to (A) exile (B) wear the letter A (C) death (D) being branded on the forehead.

_____ 3. Chillingworth is the name that is used by Hester's (A) father (B) physician (C) pastor (D) husband.

_____ 4. Arthur Dimmesdale is (A) intellectually brilliant (B) weak and sickly (C) respected by the community (D) all of the above.

_____ 5. Hester earns her living as a (A) seamstress (B) cleaning lady (C) librarian (D) soap- and candlemaker.

_____ 6. Whom does the following quote describe? "She was lady-like too, after the manner of the feminine gentility of those days; characterized by a certain state and dignity." (A) Hester (B) Mistress Hibbins (C) Pearl (D) the governor's wife.

_____ 7. Who or what is being described? "It was the scarlet letter endowed with life." (A) Pearl (B) Hester (C) Dimmesdale's tombstone (D) the letter that Hester wore on her breast.

_____ 8. Who did the following? "Holding his hand over his heart as was his custom, whenever his peculiarly nervous temperment was thrown into agitation." (A) Chillingworth (B) Bellingham (C) Winthrop (D) Dimmesdale.

_____ 9. Who is described in the following way? "At first his expression had been calm, meditative, scholarlike. Now there was something ugly and evil in his face which they had not previously noticed." (A) the sea captain (B) Chillingworth (C) Dimmesdale (D) the Apostle Eliot.

_____ 10. Who did the following? "He has violated in cold blood the sanctity of a human heart." (A) Bellingham (B) Dimmesdale (C) Chillingworth (D) Winthrop.

Name _____   Date _____

The Scarlet Letter by Nathaniel Hawthorne

Answer each of the following questions in two or three complete sentences.

1. How is the community wrong in the way that it treats Hester and Pearl?

    _____
    _____
    _____
    _____

2. How does Hester's relationship with the town change as the years pass?

    _____
    _____
    _____
    _____

3. What does Chillingworth's search for revenge do to him?

    _____
    _____
    _____
    _____

4. What happens to Dimmesdale because of his guilt?

    _____
    _____
    _____

5. Why is the third scaffold scene the most important scene in the novel?

    _____
    _____
    _____
    _____

Challenge

Why is *The Scarlet Letter* often called the first significant psychological novel in American literature?

Great Books for Independent Reading

Name _____ Date _____

The Country of the Pointed Firs by Sarah Orne Jewett

Correctly complete each sentence with information from the novel.

1. The town where the story is set is called _____.

2. The narrator goes to the village in order to _____.

3. Almira Todd specializes in _____.

4. Captain Littlepage tells the visitor _____.

5. The narrator enjoys her visit with Mrs. Blackett and William because _____

    _____.

6. During their visit to Green Island, Mrs. Todd tells her friend the story of _____

    _____.

7. The visitor rents the abandoned schoolhouse so she _____.

8. Mrs. Todd enjoys a visit with her friend, _____.

9. Mrs. Todd's main competitor in the village was _____.

10. Mrs. Todd's cousin Joanna had chosen to live alone on Shell-Heap Island because

    _____.

11. During her visit to Shell-Heap Island, the narrator felt _____.

12. Mrs. Todd and her friend make a long trip to _____.

13. The aspects of the family reunion that the visitor enjoys most are _____.

14. Elijah Tilley talks with the visitor about _____.

15. William's girlfriend Esther is a _____.

16. Mrs. Todd and the narrator visit an old lady who believes she is a twin to _____

    _____.

17. The narrator attends the wedding of _____.

18. Esther carries a _____ to her wedding.

19. The story ends as the narrator _____.

20. Mrs. Todd's parting gifts to the summer visitor include _____.

©1986, 1991 J. Weston Walch, Publisher

Great Books for Independent Reading

Name _____ Date _____

The Country of the Pointed Firs by Sarah Orne Jewett

Answer each of the following questions in two or three complete sentences.

1. Describe the unique features of Dunnet Landing and the surrounding territory.

   _____

   _____

   _____

   _____

2. What are some of the great strengths of Almira Todd's personality?

   _____

   _____

   _____

   _____

3. Every small village has a few local characters. Who are some of the very odd characters in Dunnet Landing?

   _____

   _____

   _____

   _____

4. What makes Mrs. Blackett such a very special person?

   _____

   _____

   _____

   _____

5. How does the city-bred narrator change as a result of the time that she spends at the Landing?

   _____

   _____

   _____

   _____

Challenge

Discuss some of the important values of life that the city girl learns from Dunnet Landing and its people.

Great Books for Independent Reading

Name _____ Date _____

Doctor Zhivago by Boris Pasternak

Select the letter of the word or phrase that correctly completes each statement.

_____ 1. The novel opens with the death of (A) Yuri's father (B) Yuri's mother (C) the Tzar (D) Lara's father.

_____ 2. One witness to the suicide of Yuri's father was (A) Misha Gordon (B) Uncle Nikolai (C) Yuri (D) Mr. Gromeko.

_____ 3. A first sign of the approaching revolution was a massive strike by the (A) railroad workers (B) university students (C) dock workers (D) members of the army.

_____ 4. At the Sventitsky's Christmas party, Lara (A) meets Yuri (B) first meets Komarovsky (C) tries to shoot Komarovsky (D) becomes engaged to Pasha.

_____ 5. After their marriage, Lara and Pasha (A) work on the farm (B) teach school (C) work for the Communist party (D) do hospital work.

_____ 6. An important weather symbol which recurs in the novel is (A) rain (B) sunset (C) snow (D) fog.

_____ 7. After the revolution, Yuri takes his family out of Moscow (A) by train (B) so they can get enough to eat (C) to the estate of Tonia's grandfather (D) all of the above.

_____ 8. The military conflict which ravaged the Russian people was primarily between (A) the Tzar and the peasants (B) rival communist factions (C) Russia and Germany (D) Russia and Japan.

_____ 9. On the estate and Varykino, the family lived mainly by (A) Yuri's selling poetry (B) farming (C) the help of a friend who had government connections (D) cutting lumber.

_____ 10. In Yuriatin, Yuri again sees Lara (A) in the hospital (B) on the street (C) in the library (D) at the railroad station.

_____ 11. On his way back to Tonia and his son, Yuri (A) changes his mind and returns to Lara (B) is captured (C) is shot (D) meets Lara's husband.

_____ 12. One of the cruelest revolutionary commanders is (A) Yuri's brother (B) Lara's husband (C) the son of Zhivago's estate manager (D) Tonia's cousin.

_____ 13. Yuri escapes from the rebel camp (A) on skis (B) in the back of a truck (C) by stealing a horse (D) disguised as a woman.

_____ 14. Lara's letter tells Yuri that (A) her husband is still alive (B) Yuri has a daughter (C) his family has gone back to Moscow (D) all of the above.

_____ 15. Yuri and Lara spend their happiest time (A) in her apartment (B) in Varykino (C) in Moscow (D) in the forest near Yuriatin.

16. Yuri's family was deported to (A) Berlin (B) London (C) Paris (D) Siberia.

_____ 17. Lara and her daughter were helped to escape by (A) Yuri (B) Komarovsky (C) Strelnikov (D) Misha Gordon.

_____ 18. Before his death, Lara's husband (A) confesses his crimes (B) apologizes to Yuri (C) is reunited with his wife (D) is assured of his wife's love.

_____ 19. The last writing that Yuri Zhivago did was (A) poems (B) novels (C) political pamphlets (D) plays.

_____ 20. Lara (A) later met Yuri's wife (B) was never seen in Moscow again (C) did not know of Yuri's death (D) probably died in a concentration camp.

Name _____   Date _____

Doctor Zhivago by Boris Pasternak

Answer each of the following questions in two or three complete sentences.

1. In what ways did Lara and Yuri both have very troubled childhood experiences?

    _____

    _____

    _____

    _____

2. What experiences of Zhivago's showed his very poetic reaction to nature?

    _____

    _____

    _____

    _____

3. What hardships did the Zhivago family experience on their train trip to the country?

    _____

    _____

    _____

    _____

4. When he was captured, why had Yuri decided to leave Lara and return to Tonia?

    _____

    _____

    _____

    _____

5. Why are Yuri and Lara so happy during their final days together?

    _____

    _____

    _____

    _____

Challenge

Write an essay explaining how *Doctor Zhivago* portrays both the personal revolution of an individual and the general revolution of the Russian nation.

Great Books for Independent Reading

Name _____ Date _____

The Winthrop Woman by Anya Seton

In the numbered blanks at the left, write the letter of the matching person or place.

_____ 1.	Son-in-law who accused Elizabeth of adultery with Hallet	A. Harry
_____ 2.	Elizabeth's father who was an apothecary	B. Jack
_____ 3.	Elizabeth's first husband	C. Groton
_____ 4.	Weak man who went mad because of his guilty feelings about his past	D. John Winthrop
_____ 5.	Had been the boyhood companion of an English nobleman	E. Mirabelle Gardiner
_____ 6.	Dutchwoman who was Elizabeth's neighbor and close friend	F. Telaka
_____ 7.	Autocratic head of the Winthrop family	G. Robert Feake
_____ 8.	Indian who spared Elizabeth's life because she had once saved him	H. Toby Feake
_____ 9.	Governor who arranged for Elizabeth's marriage to Hallet	I. Margaret
_____ 10.	Elizabeth's beloved aunt and substitute mother	J. Monakewaygo
_____ 11.	Gypsy who told Elizabeth that she would spend her life searching after freedom	K. Thomas Lyon
_____ 12.	Boatman who transported the family from Massachusetts Bay to Greenwich	L. Keofferam
_____ 13.	Elizabeth's jilted fiancé	M. William Hallet
_____ 14.	English country estate of the Winthrop family	N. Peyto
_____ 15.	Military captain who died defending Elizabeth and Hallet	O. Anne Hutchinson
_____ 16.	Woman who was excommunicated for her belief in a theology of grace and inner light	P. Anneke Patrick
_____ 17.	Connecticut peninsula very special to Elizabeth	Q. Daniel Patrick
_____ 18.	Elizabeth's worldly companion on the voyage to Massachusetts	R. Stuyvesant
_____ 19.	Most beloved of the Winthrop sons	S. Thomas Fones
_____ 20.	Elizabeth's Indian servant and friend	T. Edward Howes

Name _____ Date _____

The Winthrop Woman by Anya Seton

Answer each of the following questions in two or three complete sentences.

1. Why did Elizabeth find Harry and his friends so fascinating?

    _____

    _____

    _____

    _____

2. What character traits did Elizabeth have, even in her childhood, which were very unsuitable for a proper Puritan matron?

    _____

    _____

    _____

    _____

3. What political difficulties did John Winthrop have in the Massachusetts Bay Colony?

    _____

    _____

    _____

    _____

4. Why were Elizabeth and Robert Feake forced to leave Massachusetts Bay?

    _____

    _____

    _____

    _____

5. What difficulties did Elizabeth and Hallet have in legally becoming husband and wife?

    _____

    _____

    _____

    _____

    _____

Challenge

Discuss why Elizabeth Winthrop was a survivor. How did she battle against the authoritarian systems and the physical difficulties of her society?

Name _____ Date _____

Exodus by Leon Uris

In the numbered blanks at the left, write the letter of the matching person, place, or thing.

_____ 1. Term for a native-born Jewish Palestinian	A. Haj Amin
_____ 2. First document which promised the Jews a homeland in Palestine	B. Jordana
	C. Foster J. MacWilliams
_____ 3. Ally of Hitler, led the Arab hate–campaign against the Jews	D. Maccabees
	E. Kibbutz
_____ 4. American nurse who wanted to stay neutral in the conflict	F. Sabra
	G. Sutherland
_____ 5. Ship loaded with children that forced the British to give in	H. Mossad Aliyah Bet
	I. Akiva
_____ 6. Walked from Russia to Palestine	J. Exodus
_____ 7. Retired British general who settled in Palestine and aided the Jewish cause	K. Ari Ben Canaan
	L. Gan Dafna
_____ 8. Survived the ghetto of Warsaw and the Nazi concentration camps	M. Balfour Declaration
	N. Mark Parker
_____ 9. Jewish terrorist society	O. Yakov and Jossi Rabinsky
_____ 10. Female warrior who trained Jewish children in the art of self–defense	P. Karen Hansen Clemett
	Q. Dov Landau
_____ 11. Leader of the diplomatic negotiations which helped to create the state of Israel	R. Barak Ben Canaan
	S. David Ben Ami
_____ 12. Head of the Jewish terrorist organization	T. Kitty Fremont
_____ 13. Communal farms established to reclaim land in Palestine	
_____ 14. Children's settlement in Galilee where Karen and Kitty lived	
_____ 15. German Jewish girl who was hidden by a Danish Christian family	
_____ 16. Worked in an airlift operation to bring Jews to Palestine	
_____ 17. Organization for illegal Jewish immigration	
_____ 18. Engineered the mass breakout from the Acre jail	
_____ 19. Gave his life building a road to lift the seige of Jerusalem	
_____ 20. Journalist whose story from Cyprus brought the plight of the refugee children to the attention of the world	

Great Books for Independent Reading

Name _____ Date _____

Exodus by Leon Uris

Answer each of the following questions in two or three complete sentences.

1. Why did Kitty want so much to take Karen to America?

     _____

     _____

     _____

     _____

2. What were some of the impossible odds facing the Jewish settlers in Palestine?

     _____

     _____

     _____

     _____

3. How does the situation of Taha and the village of Abu Yesha illustrate the human tragedy of the conflict between the Arabs and the Jews?

     _____

     _____

     _____

     _____

4. How did Ari run the *Exodus* operation right under the noses of the British?

     _____

     _____

     _____

     _____

5. How did Dov learn survival? How did Karen help him learn to love?

     _____

     _____

     _____

     _____

Challenge

Write an essay explaining whether Leon Uris is biased or objective in the historical material which he presents. Is Uris too pro-Jewish, and too anti-British and anti-Arab? Does his bias weaken or strengthen the total effectiveness of the novel?

Name _____ Date _____

The Friendly Persuasion by Jessamyn West

Place a (+) before each statement that is true and a (0) before each statement that is false.

_____ 1. Jess Birdwell is a Quaker minister.

_____ 2. Mattie showed the same talent for playing the organ that Eliza did.

_____ 3. Enoch was the youngest of the Birdwell's sons.

_____ 4. The Birdwells had one daughter who died in childhood.

_____ 5. Eliza tended to be more superstitious and poetic than Jess did.

_____ 6. When Samantha became Eliza's pet, Jess was caught in a conflict between his love for his wife and his hatred for geese.

_____ 7. Labe understood better than Josh did that Old Alf needed someone to talk to.

_____ 8. To Mattie, Eliza's wedding ring made a sound which represented happiness and marriage.

_____ 9. Josh was wounded by a rifle bullet at the Battle of Finney's Ford.

_____ 10. The Birdwell farm was raided by Morgan's troops.

_____ 11. The buried Bible page represented a link with the Birdwell family past.

_____ 12. Lady was a better-looking horse than Red Rover was.

_____ 13. Eliza got just as emotionally involved in the race with Rev. Godley's horse as Jess did.

_____ 14. Eliza would not let Lafe Millspaugh eat at her table because Lafe refused to wash.

_____ 15. Jess was a great believer in modern, progressive innovations.

_____ 16. Jess realized the state of his own good health when he saw the problems and illnesses of others.

_____ 17. Eliza had done all of the painting on her special vase early one morning when she was first married.

_____ 18. Jess and Eliza were pleased with all of their children's choices of husbands and wives.

_____ 19. "The Illumination" refers in part to Jess's installing of inside electricity.

_____ 20. Before Jess met Homer, Eliza had already died.

©1986, 1991 J. Weston Walch, Publisher

Great Books for Independent Reading

Name _____ Date _____

The Friendly Persuasion by Jessamyn West

Answer each of the following questions in two or three complete sentences.

1. What traits of Jess's were not quite in keeping with his Quaker beliefs?

    _____

    _____

    _____

    _____

2. In what ways is Eliza both a practical woman and a woman of deep feeling?

    _____

    _____

    _____

    _____

3. What lesson does Jess learn when he acquires Lady, the mare?

    _____

    _____

    _____

    _____

4. What conflict did Josh Birdwell face when he thought that Morgan's raiders were approaching his home?

    _____

    _____

    _____

    _____

5. How does Jess's occupation as a nurseryman increase his sensitivity to life?

    _____

    _____

    _____

    _____

Challenge

Write an essay describing three objects which have great meaning in Jess and Eliza's married life. Explain the significance of each object.

Name _____   Date _____

The Caine Mutiny Court-Martial by Herman Wouk

Correctly complete each sentence with information from the novel.

1. Maryk's position on the *Caine* was _____.

2. The *Caine*'s job in the Navy was _____.

3. Greenwald took the job defending Maryk because _____

   _____.

4. The lawyer for the prosecution was _____.

5. Maryk had taken command of the *Caine* during _____.

6. Keefer's occupation in civilian life was as a _____.

7. Maryk had kept a log of _____.

8. When they went to present the information to the admiral, Keefer _____

   _____.

9. Keith accused Queeg of _____.

10. Queeg had forced Keith to pay for _____.

11. The men said that in landing the Marine forces, Queeg had _____

    _____.

12. Greenwald forces Dr. Lundeen to label Queeg's personality as _____.

13. Besides Maryk himself, the only witness that the defense called was _____.

14. The psychiatrists labeled Queeg as very _____.

15. Maryk obtained most of his knowledge of psychology from _____.

16. Greenwald gets Maryk acquitted by _____.

17. Queeg said that he had been harsh with his men in order to _____.

18. The judge refuses to _____.

19. The party in the last scene is to celebrate _____.

20. Greenwald says that the one most guilty of destructive behavior is _____.

Name _____ Date _____

The Caine Mutiny Court-Martial by Herman Wouk

Answer each of the following questions in two or three complete sentences.

1. Why did Queeg's crew dislike him so intensely?

    _____

    _____

    _____

    _____

2. According to Dr. Bird, how did Captain Queeg's navy command compensate for his psychological problems?

    _____

    _____

    _____

    _____

3. What did the captain do to make Maryk take control of the *Caine?*

    _____

    _____

    _____

    _____

4. How did Keefer use Maryk to get even with Queeg?

    _____

    _____

    _____

    _____

5. Why did Greenwald feel that officers like Queeg were important to the Navy?

    _____

    _____

    _____

    _____

Challenge

Write an essay describing how Queeg's appearance on the witness stand wins for Maryk the verdict of not guilty.

Answer Keys

Elizabeth the Queen by Maxwell Anderson

OBJECTIVE:

1. Penelope
2. Raleigh, Cecil
3. his silver armor
4. Cadiz
5. wage war against Spain
6. Bacon
7. Ireland
8. ambition, pride
9. Essex and her throne
10. her ring
11. they are intercepted
12. disband his army
13. Essex controls the city
14. king
15. has him arrested
16. Essex to send the ring
17. Shakespeare (*Henry IV*)
18. pardon Essex
19. Elizabeth
20. Penelope

SHORT ANSWER:

1. Plots by the Raleigh faction to discredit Essex.
2. His ego. He will not defer to Raleigh.
3. Temper tantrums, fear for her throne.
4. Cheers of the populace—that Essex may be set up as king.
5. His pride—he will not take anything from anyone.

CHALLENGE:

Issue of love for Essex vs. her desire for power. She keeps her throne, but loses the man she loves.

Becket by Jean Anouilh

OBJECTIVE:

1. J
2. A
3. T
4. O
5. B
6. I
7. E
8. M
9. D
10. K
11. G
12. Q
13. S
14. C
15. R
16. F
17. N
18. H
19. P
20. L

SHORT ANSWER:

1. Cares for the suffering of the people.
2. Admires the monk's spirit—sees himself as he might have been.
3. Gives away his wealth and devotes his life to God.
4. Finds a cause to die for.
5. Confused, still caring deeply for Becket, but determined to keep his crown.

CHALLENGE:

Change is greatest in Becket from sensual man to holy man as he defends the honor of God. Henry remains basically stubborn and still dependent and uncertain.

A Tale of Two Cities by Charles Dickens

OBJECTIVE:

1. J
2. R
3. A
4. O
5. D
6. H
7. M
8. S
9. B
10. I
11. N
12. K
13. Q
14. C
15. L
16. F
17. P
18. G
19. E
20. G

ANSWER KEYS (continued)

A Tale of Two Cities by Charles Dickens (continued)

SHORT ANSWER:
1. To tell her that her father has been found.
2. Stryver gets credit for all of Carton's work.
3. Darnay wants change—uncle enjoys all of the evils of class privilege.
4. He is a very gentle, caring person.
5. Threatens to reveal Basard's identity—gets Darnay out by drugging him.

CHALLENGE:
Carton gives his life. Darnay risks his life for Gabelle. Miss Pross sacrifices her hearing to save Lucy.

April Morning by Howard Fast

OBJECTIVE:

1. twenty-four hours
2. argue
3. Levi
4. his grandmother
5. signing the muster book
6. Jonas Parker
7. blacksmith
8. the reverend
9. Moses Cooper
10. the Metonomy Road
11. Solomon Chandler
12. behind rock walls
13. Joseph Simmons
14. fowling pieces, rifles
15. a British private
16. fell asleep
17. Boston
18. Ruth Simmons
19. candles
20. the siege of Boston

SHORT ANSWER:
1. He constantly found fault.
2. Puts his arm around Adam's shoulder and holds him.
3. Talk to the British. The British shot first.
4. So the British would be totally driven out.
5. Change from a boy into a man who could face responsibility.

CHALLENGE:
Involvement in other battles—Bunker Hill, etc. Marriage to Ruth, seeing a new nation founded after the Revolution.

Cimarron by Edna Ferber

OBJECTIVE:

1. D	6. B	11. B	16. C
2. D	7. B	12. D	17. C
3. B	8. A	13. A	18. B
4. D	9. C	14. D	19. C
5. B	10. C	15. A	20. D

SHORT ANSWER:
1. Girl to whom he gave a drink stole it.
2. Flashy dress, ability to shoot, court defense, preaching.
3. Brought up the children, ran the paper, built the family a place in society.
4. Donna married for money, Cim married an Indian.
5. Instant wealth totally turned social values upside down.

CHALLENGE:
Yancy—flashy daring in the middle of every adventure. Sabra—the steady work that built the country.

ANSWER KEYS *(continued)*

The Great Gatsby by F. Scott Fitzgerald

OBJECTIVE:

1. Nick
2. moves in next door
3. yawning constantly
4. a little fool
5. loud, lavish, crowded, impersonal
6. Valley of Ashes, Dr. T.J. Eckleberg
7. light on Daisy's dock
8. homely, plain, middle class
9. Tom and Myrtle fight
10. Jordan
11. Daisy and Gatsby's courtship
12. her parents refused
13. where it came from
14. Daisy and Gatsby, his house
15. Gatsby's shirts
16. Dan
17. Gatsby's car
18. Tom is with Jordan
19. Daisy, Gatsby
20. he thought Gatsby killed his wife

SHORT ANSWER:

1. They do what they want—don't care who they hurt.
2. Sees the fakeness of the lifestyle.
3. Real name Jay Gatz, no war record, money came from bootlegging.
4. Crude careless bully vs. the caring and refined gentleman.
5. No one came—empty pool vs. the night of the brightly lighted party and the house full of people.

CHALLENGE:

No real depth of human relationships, excessive craze of the jazz-age parties, desolation of the Valley, fight scene in the city apartment, Jordan's indifference.

Johnny Tremain by Esther Forbes

OBJECTIVE:

1. C
2. B
3. B
4. B
5. D
6. C
7. A
8. A
9. C
10. D
11. B
12. A
13. C
14. A
15. C
16. A
17. B
18. C
19. A
20. A

SHORT ANSWER:

1. Pouring silver into a crucible that cracked.
2. Sullen, idle, restless.
3. Messenger, eavesdropper, spy.
4. Mother was Lyte's niece.
5. To stand up proudly and not be put down by any oppressor.

CHALLENGE:

British as human—Sgt. Gale and Lt. Stranger had jobs they didn't want to do. Happy Rab was killed, Lapham girls separated.

ANSWER KEYS (continued)

The Lion in Winter by William Goldman

OBJECTIVE:

1. D	6. E	11. K	16. O
2. H	7. J	12. B	17. J
3. I	8. M	13. L	18. H
4. N	9. F	14. E	19. G
5. A	10. I	15. C	20. P

SHORT ANSWER:

1. Constant political maneuvers and verbal barbs.
2. Marriage to her as a key to land and power.
3. No one mentions him as king.
4. Her freedom and Henry's love.
5. He will let Eleanor out again for Easter Court.

CHALLENGE:

Deep feelings underneath the barbs, her seen with the jewels, the pleasure both of them find in playing the game.

The House of the Seven Gables by Nathaniel Hawthorne

OBJECTIVE:

1. A	6. C	11. D	16. A
2. A	7. B	12. C	17. C
3. C	8. D	13. D	18. A
4. A	9. C	14. B	19. D
5. D	10. C	15. C	20. B

SHORT ANSWER:

1. Old, musty, shriveled.
2. Maule cursed Pyncheon after the Colonel stole Maule's land.
3. Brings light, beauty, and youth into the house.
4. Clifford took the blame for some of Jaffrey's crooked business dealings.
5. Holgrave a descendant of Maule—he and Phoebe unite the two families. Uncle Venner represents comic-relief view of common people.

CHALLENGE:

Judge's death, retribution for the sins of his ancestors. Clifford and Hepzibah victims of the family curse. Spell broken when Phoebe and Holgrave leave.

The Scarlet Letter by Nathaniel Hawthorne

OBJECTIVE:

1. C	6. A
2. B	7. A
3. D	8. D
4. D	9. B
5. A	10. C

ANSWER KEYS (continued)

The Scarlet Letter by Nathaniel Hawthorne (continued)

SHORT ANSWER:
1. Passed judgment on her heart, not on her actions.
2. They come to accept her, but she withdraws from them.
3. Turns him into a devil.
4. Total physical and mental breakdown.
5. Dimmesdale finally becomes free of his guilt.

CHALLENGE:

Dimmesdale and Chillingworth are physically destroyed by hidden guilt. Hester's beauty fades. For each character, the outside becomes a reflection of the person's inner condition.

The Country of the Pointed Firs by Sarah Orne Jewett

OBJECTIVE:
1. Dunnet Landing
2. write
3. herbs and medicines
4. about his travels
5. simple and peaceful life
6. her love for Nathan
7. can be alone
8. Mrs. Fosdick
9. Dr. Bassett
10. her lover was lost at sea
11. very close to Joanna's spirit
12. the Bowden family reunion
13. conversation and visits with people along the way
14. his dead wife
15. a shepherdess
16. Queen Victoria
17. William and Esther
18. lamb
19. leaves the village
20. some herbs, a coral pin that Nathan had brought home

SHORT ANSWER:
1. Small, peaceful coastal community, small harbor, bay full of boats.
2. Knowledge of herbs, great understanding of human nature.
3. William, Elijah Tilley, Captain Littlepage.
4. Simple spirit and totally peaceful environment.
5. Spiritual beauty, real values of life.

CHALLENGE:

Various characters represent faithfulness in love, strong family ties, links with the values of the past.

Doctor Zhivago by Boris Pasternak

OBJECTIVE:
1. B
2. A
3. A
4. C
5. B
6. C
7. D
8. B
9. C
10. C
11. B
12. B
13. A
14. D
15. B
16. C
17. B
18. D
19. C
20. D

SHORT ANSWER:
1. Yuri lost his mother, his father disappeared. Lara was victimized by her mother's lover.
2. Beauty of the countryside in all seasons. Groves of woods, fields, snowstorms.
3. Hunger, thirst, filth, crowded conditions.
4. Sense of loyalty and duty.
5. Find private peace in an outer world that is coming apart.

ANSWER KEYS (continued)

Doctor Zhivago by Boris Pasternak (continued)

CHALLENGE:

Yuri and Lara lose and find each other against the background of the social upheaval in Russia. They are finally parted forever by those same social currents.

The Winthrop Woman by Anya Seton

OBJECTIVE:

1. K	6. P	11. N	16. O
2. S	7. D	12. H	17. J
3. A	8. L	13. T	18. E
4. G	9. R	14. C	19. B
5. M	10. I	15. Q	20. F

SHORT ANSWER:

1. Exciting worldly life versus dull Puritanism.
2. Strong, independent personality, love of color, excitement, and adventure.
3. His authority was opposed, the Dudley faction, lost elections, the oppositions of Roger Williams and Anne Hutchinson.
4. Involvement in the Hutchinson affair, accusation of witchcraft.
5. Problems with Feake, opposition of son-in-law, caught in currents of New Amsterdam's politics.

CHALLENGE:

Survived Harry's death, built family and lands despite Feake's weakness, unfulfilled love for Jack, support for Anne Hutchinson, is finally able to marry Hallet.

Exodus by Leon Uris

OBJECTIVE:

1. F	6. O	11. R	16. C
2. M	7. G	12. I	17. H
3. A	8. Q	13. E	18. K
4. T	9. D	14. L	19. S
5. J	10. B	15. P	20. N

SHORT ANSWER:

1. To save Karen from the past, to provide a substitute for the daughter that Kitty had lost.
2. Swamps and rocky land, no social structure, Arab problems, British domination.
3. Friends who had lived together became enemies who fought each other.
4. Stole trucks and uniforms, looked like a genuine British army division.
5. Learned survival in the ghettos and concentration camps. Karen taught Dov to love again.

CHALLENGE:

Uris a pro-Jewish position. Frequently anti-British. Individual characters' actions are strengthened by their beliefs. All are caught in the cross-currents of political and military events.

ANSWER KEYS (continued)

The Friendly Persuasion by Jessamyn West (continued)

OBJECTIVE:

1.	0	6.	+	11.	+	16.	+
2.	0	7.	+	12.	0	17.	0
3.	0	8.	+	13.	+	18.	0
4.	+	9.	0	14.	0	19.	0
5.	0	10.	0	15.	+	20.	0

SHORT ANSWER:

1. Love of music, poetry, fast horses.
2. Excellent homemaker, deeply religious and loving.
3. Appearance is not everything.
4. His Quaker religious beliefs versus the desire to defend his home.
5. Noticed changes of seasons, land, natural beauty.

CHALLENGE:

The vase Eliza had painted, the page from the old family Bible, the wedding ring as a symbol of marriage and maturity.

The Caine Mutiny Court-Martial by Herman Wouk

OBJECTIVE:

1. executive officer
2. a mine sweeper
3. he was ordered to do so
4. Challee
5. a typhoon
6. a novelist
7. Queeg's strange behavior
8. chickened out
9. cruelty to his men
10. a case of liquor
11. taken the ship away too soon
12. paranoid
13. Queeg
14. disturbed
15. Keefer's psychology books
16. breaking down Queeg
17. enforce discipline
18. censure Greenwald
19. publication of Keefer's book
20. Keefer

SHORT ANSWER:

1. Unnecessarily hard on his men for foolish details, punishments too strict for the offenses.
2. By being the absolute authority on his ship.
3. Refused to turn the ship around in a storm.
4. Keefer gave information which made Maryk believe that Queeg was unbalanced.
5. Maintained discipline and helped keep the country's military defenses strong.

CHALLENGE:

Greenwald battered Queeg on the witness stand until the court was convinced that the Captain was mentally unbalanced.

Unit 3
Questions of Conscience

Synopses

To Sir With Love
by E.R. Braithwaite

This special story of student-teacher relationships takes place at Greenslade School in London's East End shortly after World War II. Rick Braithwaite cannot get a job as an engineer because he is black. He obtains a job teaching Greenslade's "incorrigibles." This experience changes his life and theirs. "Sir" teaches his students manners, gives them an appreciation for cultures and peoples outside their own, and helps the young adults gain self-respect. Encouraged by his principal, Mr. Florian, "Sir's" teaching tools range from ballet to boxing. The most powerful lessons, however, come from the students' own lives. A young girl grows into a woman by understanding the needs of her mother. The class stands against the racial prejudice of the community to attend the funeral of a black classmate's father. "Sir," in turn, must deal with his own feelings as he falls in love with Gillian, who is white, and must consider if their love is strong enough to withstand the forces that will attack their marriage. This book illustrates the truth that a good teacher both helps students to learn and in turn learns from his or her students.

The Good Earth
by Pearl S. Buck

This epic novel of China in the early nineteenth century traces the rise of Wang Lung's family from peasant to patrician status. Wang and his wife O-lan survive famine, flood, and war to retain the land, which represents to them the source of life. But as Wang's family builds a financial empire, their simple ways are corrupted by the civilization of the city. Wang fails as a parent, and his sons move further from mother earth. The simple values which made the family great are adulterated by greed and the lust for power. Wang himself rejects his faithful wife and becomes infatuated with a beautiful young courtesan. At the end of the novel, Wang's sons stand ready to destroy everything their father has built. Old Wang himself simply wants to return to the land. The author pictures powerfully the survival struggle of the people of China, the values of the simple life, and the corrupting dangers of luxury.

The Chocolate War
by Robert Cormier

Can one individual's rebellion defeat a corrupt system and "dare to disturb the universe?" Jerry Renault, the new boy at Trinity School, accepts his assignment from the Vigils, the school's gang of controllers. He is not to participate in the school's annual chocolate sale. Brother Leon, the school's assistant headmaster, is using the Vigils and their leader Archie Costello in Leon's own drive for power. The authority figures that Cormier pictures are less than ideal role models. Leon is vicious and Brother Eugene is weak. Only Brother Jacques acts to save Jerry from being totally destroyed. The students represent a cross section of human attitudes. The helpless Goober runs away instead of standing up to help Jerry. Totally corrupt Emile Janza, who defiles everything that he touches, is disgusting even to Archie. Jerry Renault dares to defy the system as one man's act of courage. Although Jerry loses his battle, the loner gains nobility as he stands up for what he believes in, even against crushing odds.

I Am the Cheese
by Robert Cormier

As shy, sensitive Adam Farmer bicycles to Vermont to visit his father, the mystery of Adam's past is unraveled. The novel's main story is told through a series of flashbacks. Adam's family had to assume a new identity when his father, a newspaper man, had become a government witness against a crime syndicate. Adam finds out the truth about himself as he is able to link his own memories with a birth certificate in a locked drawer and an overheard phone call. Adam's closest friend, Amy Hertz, brightens the serious side of Adam's nature. But is Amy real? Why is Dr. Brint asking so many questions? Was the mysterious Mr. Gray friend or enemy? Adam himself is now threatened by the evil forces that destroyed his family. Cormier has woven a clever plot by using three different levels of narrative: the bike trip, the interviews with Dr. Brint, and Adam's own memories. This book, like many of Cormier's other novels, has a hero who must struggle against the system. As in the nursery rhyme that his father had sung to him, Adam Farmer becomes the "cheese who stands alone."

The Autobiography of Miss Jane Pittman
by Ernest J. Gaines

This story of one black woman's courageous fight for life and dignity begins during the Civil War and ends during the civil rights demonstrations of the 1960s. Miss Jane, at age 110, tells her own story. Jane and Ned, the child of a black woman killed by Yankee soldiers, escape from the plantation in the aftermath of the Union Army's march through the South. Although she is no longer a slave, Miss Jane lives in the Negro quarters and works as a cook in Mr. Samson's kitchen. Joe Pittman, the man she loves, is killed by a horse. Racial violence claims the life of her adopted son Ned as the young man is trying to build a better life for his people. This novel shows how any reform movement in the first half of the twentieth century was feared by the blacks. The slave mentality still made them fear that their white employers would take away their meager wages, food, and housing. Robert Samson, the young master on the estate, becomes a victim of the South's racial standards. He falls in love with Mary Agnes, a girl with the "taint" of black blood. Despair eventually drives Robert to suicide. Young Jimmy brings new hope to the people of the plantation. He also is killed before the demonstrations that he has planned can take place. After Jimmy's death, Miss Jane, then over one hundred years old, participates in the protest action to give blacks the right to drink at public fountains. Miss Jane's singular life illustrates a century of struggle by black Americans from the chains of slavery to the rights of full citizenship.

Black Like Me
by John Howard Griffin

Journalist John Griffin changes his skin color from white to black by using medication and sun lamp treatments. He then ventures into the deep South during the 1960s to find out how a black man really feels. Griffin begins in New Orleans, a city in which he finds some tolerance. He journeys across the South to Atlanta. The worst experiences of hatred come in Mississippi. Things that a white man would take for granted—getting a drink of water and finding a rest room—are prohibited to a black man. Dealing with the "hate stares" of vicious whites and the loneliness of his isolation from his own family become major problems for Griffin. However, the traveler also finds kindness in a rural family who will share with a stranger their poor home and meager supply of food. Newspaper editor P.D. East agrees to print Griffin's accounts of his experiences. When the articles are published, the explosion of prejudice in Griffin's home town is so great that his family is forced to move. The autobiography shows a very ugly side of American society. In the land of the free, the way a man is treated differs only because he has changed the color of his skin.

A Raisin in the Sun
by Lorraine Hansbury

On the south side of Chicago in the 1940s, the Younger family lives in a crowded, shabby apartment. This powerful play deals with the conflicts which erupt as the family awaits the arrival of Walter Senior's insurance check. Walter Junior struggles for his dreams in a world which constantly frustrates his efforts to achieve manhood. Ruth loves her husband but cannot always understand him. Walter's sister Beneatha wants to express her individuality. She is fascinated by Asagai, a young Nigerian. Lena, the mother, desperately attempting to hold the family together, uses some of the insurance money to make a down payment on a house in an all-white neighborhood. After Walter's lack of judgment causes the loss of the rest of the money in a liquor store venture and the white neighbors threaten the family, Lena is nearly defeated. Walter is then able to assert his manhood for Travis, his young son, who represents the family's hope for the future. A powerful study of modern black Americans, this play is a wonderful story of family love and survival.

The Little Foxes
by Lillian Hellman

Do the meek inherit the earth, or do the vicious devour it? Lillian Hellman's powerful social drama shows some of these devourers at work. Regina Giddens and her brothers, Oscar and Ben Hubbard, are conspiring to make a fortune by building a cotton mill in partnership with a Chicago tycoon. Regina's ailing husband Horace blocks their plans because Horace does not want the town destroyed. Horace and Regina's daughter, Alexandra, side with her father against the Hubbards' plots. Birdie, Oscar's wife, is a pathetic alcoholic who escapes to the bottle and the memories of her girlhood on the plantation. The Hubbards' financial schemes threaten to backfire when Horace discovers that the brothers have "borrowed" some of his stock to use as collateral for their loan. Viciousness becomes personified as Regina allows Horace to die so she can get what she wants. The conspirators begin to threaten each other in attempts to get the lion's share of the money. Alexandra, at the drama's conclusion, asks Regina, "Mama, are you afraid???" This play presents the brutal world of business which seems to be controlled by characters totally lacking in conscience and ethics.

Inherit the Wind
by Jerome Laurence and Robert E. Lee

This play is a fictionalized version of the famous Scopes Monkey Trial, which pitted Clarence Darrow against William Jennings Bryan. As the drama opens, Bertram Cates is on trial in Hillsboro for teaching Darwinism in his science class. The real issue on trial is a man's right to think for himself. Two great legal giants have come to argue the case: Matthew Harrison Brady, champion of Biblical creationism, and Henry Drummond, who appears to the religious forces in the town as the Devil incarnate. Hornbeck, a cynical reporter for a Baltimore newspaper, serves as narrator for the play's action. Caught between the two powerful currents is Rachel Brown, the daughter of the town's fundamentalist minister, who is in love with Bert. The trial in the stuffy courtroom builds to a fever pitch. After all scientific evidence is rejected as irrelevant, Drummond puts Brady on the stand as a witness for the defense. Through Drummond's clever line of questioning, Brady is forced to admit that the Bible is not the only authority for truth. Brady in turn accuses Drummond of attempting to destroy people's faith. Although the court finds Bert guilty, Drummond has won his point and Brady has lost his audience. The right of choice has been much more on trial than Bert Cates has. *Inherit the Wind* is not an antireligious play. The authors make a powerful statement for the right of man to have an open mind.

To Kill a Mockingbird
by Harper Lee

This childhood memory novel is set in Maycomb, Alabama in the 1930s. Scout and Jem, the motherless children of lawyer Atticus Finch, are being brought up by Calpurnia, the motherly Negro housekeeper who will tolerate no foolishness. Scout remembers their childhood playmate Dill, who came from Mississippi each summer. She recalls the neighbors: Miss Maudie, Miss Stephanie Crawford, and cantankerous Mrs. Dubose. The magnet which drew the children's imagination was the mysterious Radley house next door. The reader sees through Scout's eyes the reactions of Maycomb's citizens when their father agrees to defend Tom Robinson, a Negro accused of raping a white girl. Scout and Jem try to defend the family honor with their fists. Their father battles a prejudiced judicial system that will convict the man because his skin is the wrong color. Harper Lee shows the evil in destroying the innocent, that it is "a sin to kill a mockingbird." In the novel's exciting conclusion, Scout's life is saved by a very unexpected friend. The author presents beautifully the relationship between Atticus and his children, the small comic episodes of the neighborhood, and the larger human issues of class and race relationships.

Main Street
by Sinclair Lewis

Nobel prize winner Lewis pictures powerfully the mental and social mediocrity of small town America in the 1920s. Idealistic librarian Carol marries Dr. Will Kennicott and moves to Gopher Prairie. The young bride has starry-eyed visions of turning the town into a cultural oasis. But Carol struggles in vain to bring reform and culture to people who do not want to change. Her marriage to Will becomes more dull with each passing year. In contrast to the Kennicott's boring marriage is the true love of Bea and Miles Bjornstam, who have been cast out by Gopher Prairie's "elite." The author's ironic style shows the readers clearly who the "best people" really are. Other victims of the vicious tongues of Gopher Prairie are Fern, the young teacher, and Erik, the sensitive artist. Carol sees in Erik the man she might have had. Although Carol escapes from the town and spends two years in Washington D.C., she eventually returns. Seeing no change in her own time, Carol hopes that things may be different for the next generation. This novel portrays "the village virus," the shallowness and apathy that Lewis saw on every main street in America.

The Crucible
by Arthur Miller

In 1693, Salem, Massachusetts was nearly destroyed by the infamous witchcraft trials. Miller's play presents this town as an example of the passions of greed, hatred, and envy which might destroy any society. The girls, led by Abigail Williams, begin to pretend that they are possessed and to accuse the town's social outcasts. As the hysteria mounts, Abigail seeks to seduce John Proctor, who has already made love to her, and to get even with John's wife Elizabeth for dismissing Abigail from her service. The town parson, Rev. Parris, is locked in a power struggle within his church. Old hatred emerges between the families of Thomas Putnam and Francis Nurse. Rev. Hale is called in as an expert on witchcraft. After he has condemned many to death, Hale realizes that the real evil in Salem lies in the hearts of its citizens. One very pathetic character is Mary Warren, who becomes Abigail's tool. Abigail reduces Mary to a hysteria which leads to John Proctor's arrest and condemnation. At the end of the drama, Proctor finds cleansing for the guilt in his own soul. Written during the McCarthy era, when hysteria was on the march in America, the play shows that a society can be corrupted when sanity is defeated and emotions are out of control.

Animal Farm
by George Orwell

Using the beast fable form, Orwell presents the communist revolution as a dream gone sour. When the animals, led by pigs Napoleon and Snowball, drive out Farmer Jones and his men, the animals have high hopes for a better life. The Animal Commandments are established as just rules for all. After Napoleon drives out Snowball and assumes authoritarian contol, conditions deteriorate. The laws are revised, with the aid of Squealer the propaganda agent, to mean what Napoleon says they mean. All dissent is brutally crushed. Even the loyal horse Boxer is sold to the glue factory when he can no longer produce. In the end, the pig rulers become exactly like the men they have driven out. Orwell personifies the animals to represent the varying attitudes toward communism and capitalism. Students would need to do some background reading on the history of the communist revolution in order to fully appreciate this book. Orwell believed at first that communism would help the working class. He wrote *Animal Farm* to show that the dream had failed.

Cry, the Beloved Country
by Alan Paton

This epic novel of South Africa, written in 1949, is crucial to a student's understanding of the problems of apartheid, the doctrine of race separation which is destroying South Africa's people. Paton weeps for a land that is being broken because the old tribal roots are disappearing. The young are being lured by the promise of wealth in the cities and in the mines. Stephen Kumalo's family is the author's example of this social breakup. Stephen goes to Johannesburg in search of his son Absalom and his sister Gertrude. Bewildered by the great city, Stephen is aided by a fellow priest, Msimangu. Stephen finds that his sister has become a prostitute. Absalom has been involved in the murder of Arthur Jarvis, son of a wealthy landowner who lives near Stephen's village. Arthur's death was particularly tragic because the young man was working for social reform to benefit both black and white South Africans. Absalom is condemned to be hanged, while the real criminals who planned the murder go free. Stephen's efforts to save his sister fail; Gertrude returns to her former life. Yet Stephen sees a ray of hope when James Jarvis sends a farm expert to help the people of the valley. Real hope for change, however, lies with the next generation, with Gertrude's child and with Arthur Jarvis' young son, "the child with brightness in him." Paton's novel presents the problems facing his country in the 1980s. The author's warning still applies: "The world cannot afford another Johannesburg."

Twelve Angry Men
by Reginald Rose

This television drama opens as a jury of ordinary men begin deliberations to decide the fate of a boy accused of knifing his father. The case seems easy. At first, one man votes "not guilty" because he feels that the case at least deserves to be discussed. The reader never knows the names of these jurors; each is just an average man with a number. As the debate continues, tempers rise. The attitudes of the jury members toward the boy reveal what kind of person each juryman is under the skin. Under closer scrutiny, the testimony of each witness and the validity of each piece of evidence is called into question. Reasonable doubt as to the boy's guilt is clearly established. This play shows the great responsibility that a person on a jury has when he or she is asked to decide the fate of another person. The drama of Rose's plot emerges as these jurymen themselves are made vulnerable by the pressures of the judicial process.

A Majority of One
by Leonard Spigelgass

Mrs. Jacoby, a Jewish lady from Brooklyn, has strong prejudices against the Japanese, who killed her son David. When Mrs. Jacoby goes to live in Japan with her daughter and son–in–law, she meets Mr. Asano, a prominent Japanese businessman. His son was also killed in the war. Two lonely people become friends when Mrs. Jacobs approaches Mr. Asano to help in her son–in–law's trade negotiations. However, when Mr. Asano asks her to keep company with him, proposing a serious relationship according to Japanese customs, Mrs. Jacoby refuses. She still thinks too much of her husband Sam to love anyone else. However, when Mr. Asano comes to New York, the two can be friends on a more casual basis. Through Mrs. Jacoby's experience, the author of the play presents the lesson that enemies can become friends. Each person can deal with the prejudices within the self, and can become a very important "majority of one."

The Hiding Place
by Corrie Ten Boom

This true story of one Dutch woman's survival in a German concentration camp shows that faith and love can conquer hate. The peaceful life of the Ten Booms, a family of watchmakers, is shattered when the Germans invade Holland. The family home becomes a hiding place for Jews who are fleeing the holocaust. Until they are captured, Corrie and her family work with the underground to save many lives. Corrie's elderly father dies at the hands of the Germans. Corrie and her sister Betsie suffer greatly, first in a Dutch prison and finally in the German camp at Ravensbruck. The two women survive through their faith in God, a faith which they share with the other prisoners. They experience many examples of human kindness in the midst of the horror. Betsie finally dies from illness and starvation. Corrie, released due to a clerical error, makes her way back home to Holland. After the war, Corrie establishes a new mission to help those whose lives had been shattered by the concentration camp experience. Corrie Ten Boom's biography shows that, even in the worst situations, people of faith can find the strength to survive and to help others.

Native Son
by Richard Wright

Bigger Thomas, a young black man living in New York in the 1930s, exists on the edge of explosive frustration. Bigger goes to work for Mr. Dalton, a wealthy philanthropist who wants to give young black boys a chance. Yet, ironically, Dalton also owns the rat–infested tenement in which Bigger and his family are forced to live. Finally the anger inside Bigger explodes. To prove his manhood, he commits two murders. He strangles Mary Dalton and shoves her body into the furnace. The crime is discovered only when one of Mary's earrings is found. As the police close in on him, Bigger also murders his mistress Bessie. The trial becomes a spectacle as the whites of Chicago erupt in rage against all blacks. Buckley, the prosecuting attorney, seeks to make an example of Bigger, and to use the racial hatred of the community to further his own political ambitions. He presents Bigger as nothing more than a vicious animal. In the novel's very didactic conclusion Richard Wright, using the summation of Max, the defense lawyer, claims that society is responsible for Bigger's crime. The black population has been dehumanized, frustrated, and forced to strike back in anger. Although rather "preachy" in some places, *Native Son* is a powerful social novel by one of America's finest black writers.

Name _____   Date _____

To Sir With Love by E.R. Braithwaite

In the numbered blanks at the left, write the letter of the matching person or place.

_____ 1. Narrator of the story

_____ 2. Supposed to be a difficult place to teach

_____ 3. Student whose father died

_____ 4. Opposite of "Sir" in appearance and attitude

_____ 5. Girl that "Sir" intended to marry

_____ 6. Domestic science teacher who understood kids

_____ 7. Developed from a girl into an attractive young woman

_____ 8. Attacked a teacher in gym class

_____ 9. Fat boy that others made fun of

_____ 10. Principal with progressive ideas

_____ 11. Taught the class before "Sir" took over

_____ 12. Defeated by "Sir" in a boxing match

_____ 13. The art teacher

_____ 14. Taught physical education

_____ 15. Stabbed a boy with an antique knife

A. Mrs. Dale-Evans
B. Mr. Florian
C. Greenslade
D. Pamela Dare
E. Denham
F. Weston
G. Buckley
H. Fernman
I. Mr. Bell
J. Rick
K. Potter
L. Gillian
M. Clinty
N. Hackman
O. Seales

Name _____ Date _____

To Sir With Love by E.R. Braithwaite

Answer each of the following questions in two or three complete sentences.

1. After Braithwaite left the service, what problems did he have in getting a job?

    _____

    _____

    _____

    _____

2. What special circumstances in the lives of the students influenced the ways that they behaved in school?

    _____

    _____

    _____

    _____

3. What did "Sir" hope to accomplish by the rules that he established for his class?

    _____

    _____

    _____

    _____

4. How did the class change in their interests and attitudes during the year that "Sir" taught them?

    _____

    _____

    _____

    _____

5. Why is Pamela Dare a good example of the growth that took place in "Sir's" students?

    _____

    _____

    _____

    _____

Challenge

A good teacher both helps his students to learn and learns from his students. Discuss the ways that *To Sir With Love* illustrates the truth of this statement.

Great Books for Independent Reading

Name _____ Date _____

The Good Earth by Pearl S. Buck

Select the letter of the word or phrase which correctly completes each statement.

_____ 1. The novel opens on (A) Wang Lung's birthday (B) the day of the great flood (C) Wang Lung's wedding day (D) the day his first son is born.

_____ 2. O-lan has all of the following characteristics except: (A) loyalty (B) physical strength (C) cooking skill (D) talkativeness.

_____ 3. The family is reduced to poverty because of (A) war (B) flood (C) drought (D) the invasion of robber bands.

_____ 4. Wang Lung is forced to sell everything except (A) his oldest daughter (B) his tools (C) his father's bed (D) his land.

_____ 5. The family travels to the South by (A) train (B) foot (C) boat (D) oxcart.

_____ 6. In the city, Wang Lung (A) is a beggar (B) works as a rickshaw carrier (C) enlists in the army (D) negotiates for the purchase of more land.

_____ 7. The gold which begins the family's new life comes from (A) selling land (B) his uncle's kindness (C) a desperate, dying rich man (D) an inheritance from his father.

_____ 8. As his lands and wealth grow, Wang's most dependable assistant is (A) his father (B) Ching (C) his eldest son (D) his uncle's son.

_____ 9. Signs of Wang's increasing prosperity include (A) his son's going to school (B) his buying land from the House of Hwang (C) his hiring laborers to work his land (D) all of the above.

_____ 10. Wang becomes infatuated with Lotus (A) when O-lan dies (B) because he has too much leisure time (C) because she reminds him of O-lan (D) because she is interested in his farming projects.

_____ 11. The reader dislikes Wang most when (A) he refuses to sell his land (B) he brings Lotus to his house (C) he takes O-lan's pearls (D) he beats up his son.

_____ 12. Wang decides that his third son (A) will be a merchant (B) will go to school (C) must remain on the land (D) will become a soldier.

_____ 13. Wang is forced to feed and house his uncle's family because (A) he fears attacks by robbers (B) he has a sense of family obligation (C) O-lan asks him to (D) it is his father's dying request.

_____ 14. The move to the great house in the city represents (A) the change in the family's social position (B) the rejection of simple values (C) the dominance of the sons over the father (D) all of the above.

_____ 15. The family's financial empire is supervised by (A) Wang's uncle (B) the second son (C) the eldest son (D) Wang himself.

_____ 16. In his last years, Wang most wanted (A) grandsons (B) peace (C) a new wife (D) more wealth.

_____ 17. The great house is almost destroyed by (A) quartered soldiers (B) a fire (C) a flood (D) an earthquake.

_____ 18. In his last years, Wang is comforted by (A) Cukoo (B) Lotus (C) Pear Blossom (D) the wife of his son.

_____ 19. Wang spends the last years of his life (A) in the great house (B) in the South (C) in his old house on the land (D) at the teahouse.

_____ 20. At the end of the novel, Wang's sons (A) openly defy their father (B) will obey their father's wishes (C) plan to destroy what Wang has built (D) show great respect for the old ways of life.

Name _____   Date _____

The Good Earth by Pearl S. Buck

Answer each of the following questions in two or three complete sentences.

1. How does O-lan give Wang Lung strength during the early years of their marriage?

    _____

    _____

    _____

    _____

2. Why will Wang Lung sacrifice everything to keep his land?

    _____

    _____

    _____

    _____

3. How does Wang's love for O-lan differ from his infatuation with Lotus?

    _____

    _____

    _____

    _____

4. How is Wang a failure as a parent?

    _____

    _____

    _____

    _____

5. By the end of the novel, how has the Lung family become exactly like the House of Hwang?

    _____

    _____

    _____

    _____

Challenge

Write an essay to show how *The Good Earth* illustrates the destructive power of wealth on individuals and human relationships. What important personal values are lost as the emphasis of life is placed on material gain?

©1986, 1991 J. Weston Walch, Publisher

Great Books for Independent Reading

Name _____   Date _____

The Chocolate War by Robert Cormier

In the numbered blanks at the left, write the letter of the matching person or place. You will use some letters more than once.

_____	1.	Brilliant student who was humiliated and accused of cheating
_____	2.	Sadistic teacher who uses his classroom to exercise his own vicious nature
_____	3.	Natural runner and athlete
_____	4.	Boy used by the Vigils to finally destroy Jerry
_____	5.	Treasurer for the chocolate campaign
_____	6.	Gave assignments for the Vigils
_____	7.	Had to help Goober complete his assignment
_____	8.	Was beaten up by Carter for defying the Vigils
_____	9.	Was forced to tell Brother Leon about Jerry's assignment
_____	10.	Had a nervous breakdown when his classroom was taken apart
_____	11.	Setting for the novel
_____	12.	Became a symbol of one man's rebellion against the system
_____	13.	President of the Vigils
_____	14.	Hardworking pharmacist
_____	15.	History teacher who had been "tipped off" by Archie
_____	16.	Might have to carry out the assignments that he gave to others
_____	17.	His mother had died of cancer
_____	18.	Stopped the fight by turning out the lights
_____	19.	Saw the chocolate campaign as a means to establish control and power
_____	20.	Quit the football team as an act of protest

A. Mr. Renault
B. Trinity
C. Frankie Rollo
D. Brother Jacques
E. Caroni
F. Brian Cochran
G. Carter
H. Janza
I. Bailey
J. Jerry Renault
K. Brother Eugene
L. Obie
M. Brother Leon
N. Archie Costello
O. Goober

Name _____ Date _____

The Chocolate War by Robert Cormier

Answer each of the following questions in two or three complete sentences.

1. Why does Jerry continue to refuse the chocolates, even after his assignment from the Vigils is over?

   _____

   _____

   _____

   _____

2. How does Brother Leon plan to use the Vigils for his own purposes?

   _____

   _____

   _____

   _____

3. What is the significance of the "black box" in the Vigils organization?

   _____

   _____

   _____

   _____

4. How is Jerry harrassed by the other students?

   _____

   _____

   _____

   _____

5. What happens at the "raffle"? How is the fight finally stopped?

   _____

   _____

   _____

   _____

Challenge

Jerry Renault is one individual who "dares to disturb the universe." Write an essay explaining how author Robert Cormier gives Jerry a dignity of human spirit, even though Jerry fails in his attempt to fight against the system.

Great Books for Independent Reading

Name _____ Date _____

I Am the Cheese by Robert Cormier

Place a (+) before each statement that is true and a (0) before each statement that is false.

_____ 1. As the story opens, Adam is riding a bus to Vermont.

_____ 2. Adam is going to see his father.

_____ 3. Adam instinctively trusts Dr. Brint because of Brint's kindly eyes.

_____ 4. Adam's earliest memories have to do with the sounds and smells of his parents.

_____ 5. During Adam's childhood, the family moved frequently.

_____ 6. Adam remembers "The Farmer in the Dell," because his father sang that song to him frequently.

_____ 7. When the dog attacks him, Adam falls from his bike and lands in the ditch.

_____ 8. Adam's father had protected him from a dog when Adam was a child.

_____ 9. Adam enjoys being with Amy because she makes him feel good about himself.

_____ 10. Every one of Amy's "Numbers" that Adam helps with is successful.

_____ 11. The visiting editor from Rawlings told Amy that he used to work with Adam's father.

_____ 12. Adam shows real courage in the restaurant when he defends the package from Junior Varney and his friends.

_____ 13. Adam learns that his family had to run and hide because Adam's father had a criminal record.

_____ 14. After he finds out the truth about his identity, Adam is very angry because his parents have lied to him.

_____ 15. The greatest fear that the family faces is the fear of the unknown.

_____ 16. Adam's parents were killed in a plane crash.

_____ 17. Amy Hertz never really existed.

_____ 18. Mr. Grey was a true friend who protected the Delmonte family.

_____ 19. On his bike trip, Adam is able to stay at the same motel where he had stayed with his parents.

_____ 20. At the end of the story, Adam and his father are reunited.

Name _____   Date _____

I Am the Cheese by Robert Cormier

Answer each of the following questions in two or three complete sentences.

1. How does Adam Farmer (Paul Delmonte) show himself to be a brave person in spite of his many fears?

    _____

    _____

    _____

    _____

2. Why is Adam's relationship with Amy Hertz so special?

    _____

    _____

    _____

    _____

3. Why did Adam's family have to assume a new identity?

    _____

    _____

    _____

    _____

4. What are some of the clues that Adam gets as he begins to learn the truth?

    _____

    _____

    _____

    _____

5. What does Adam's mother mean by the "Never-Knows"? Why are these the greatest fears of all?

    _____

    _____

    _____

    _____

Challenge

Paul Delmonte (Adam Farmer) is fighting for survival. How is this fight linked to the title of the novel? Do you believe that the boy will succeed in this struggle? Why or why not?

Name _____ Date _____

The Autobiography of Miss Jane Pittman
by Ernest J. Gaines

Place a (+) before each statement that is true and a (0) before each statement that is false.

_____ 1. When she died, Miss Jane was 110 years old.

_____ 2. As a slave, Miss Jane had been the cook on her master's plantation.

_____ 3. Most of the story takes place in Mississippi.

_____ 4. After the Emancipation Proclamation, the freed slaves received a great deal of help from the government.

_____ 5. Ned was Miss Jane's son.

_____ 6. Miss Jane was given her name by a Yankee soldier.

_____ 7. Joe Pittman was killed by a horse he was attempting to break.

_____ 8. Ned was attempting to build a school to aid Negro children.

_____ 9. Ned died in a violent flood.

_____ 10. Living conditions for the freed blacks were not much better than they had been in the days of slavery.

_____ 11. The sheriff could find no witnesses to testify to Ned's death.

_____ 12. Religion played an important part in Jane Pittman's life.

_____ 13. Mary Agnes LeFabre had a very small amount of Negro blood.

_____ 14. Robert Samson would not tolerate his son having any relationship at all with a Negro woman.

_____ 15. Mary Agnes encouraged Tee Bob's romantic advances.

_____ 16. Tee Bob shot himself.

_____ 17. Jimmy was punished less strictly because Jane and his aunt Lena felt that he had special gifts and abilities.

_____ 18. Even though Jane was too old to continue cooking for the Samson family, she continued to live in the cook's residence.

_____ 19. Robert Sampson rented most of his farm acreage to Negro sharecroppers.

_____ 20. Miss Jane particpated in a civil rights protest which centered around a public drinking fountain.

Great Books for Independent Reading

Name _____ Date _____

The Autobiography of Miss Jane Pittman
by Ernest J. Gaines

Answer each of the following questions in two or three complete sentences.

1. How did Jane and Ned survive their journey after leaving the plantation?

    _____

    _____

    _____

    _____

2. How did the whites take advantage of the ignorance of the freed blacks?

    _____

    _____

    _____

    _____

3. How did Ned Douglass try to help his people?

    _____

    _____

    _____

    _____

4. How was young Robert Samson a victim of the double standard in Southern society?

    _____

    _____

    _____

    _____

5. What did Miss Jane mean when she said that they knew that Jimmy was "the One"?

    _____

    _____

    _____

    _____

Challenge

In one speech, Ned Douglass told his audience that a black American is different from a nigger, because a black American "cares and will always struggle." Write an essay to illustrate how Miss Jane Pittman is an example of such an American.

©1986, 1991 J. Weston Walch, Publisher

Great Books for Independent Reading

Name _____   Date _____

Black Like Me by John Howard Griffin

Correctly complete each sentence with information from the novel.

1. Griffin by profession is a _____.

2. In his experiment, Griffin changed only _____.

3. The medical procedure to change the color of Griffin's skin was done in _____
    _____.

4. His skin color changed gradually by using _____

    and _____.

5. The shoeshine man in New Orleans who helped Griffin was named _____.

6. Griffin realized how totally his appearance had changed when _____
    _____.

7. His greatest physical discomforts as a black man came from not being easily able to

    find _____ and _____.

8. Griffin feels that the black man's greatest need is for _____.

9. The man lynched in Mississippi was named _____.

10. The "hate stare" was _____.

11. The "best" Negroes were thought to be _____.

12. Griffin was greatly assisted by a courageous newspaper editor named _____
    _____.

13. The men who gave Griffin rides were mostly interested in _____.

14. Griffin's most wonderful experience as a black came when _____
    _____.

15. The city where Griffin functioned both as a black and as a white was _____.

16. The magazine which first published Griffin's articles was the _____.

17. The most difficult emotional aspect of Griffin's experiment was the _____.

18. The total time that Griffin remained a Negro was about _____.

19. When they found out what Griffin had done, the people of his home town _____
    _____.

20. In order to escape the publicity, Griffin's family had to _____.

Great Books for Independent Reading

Name _____ Date _____

Black Like Me by John Howard Griffin

Answer each of the following questions in two or three complete sentences.

1. Describe the process by which Griffin became a Negro.

    _____

    _____

    _____

    _____

2. Why did Griffin make this experiment?

    _____

    _____

    _____

    _____

3. How was he treated differently as a black man in New Orleans than he was treated in Mississippi?

    _____

    _____

    _____

    _____

4. Describe the public reaction when Griffin's story was published.

    _____

    _____

    _____

    _____

5. What does Griffin believe are the greatest dangers in the modern civil rights movement?

    _____

    _____

    _____

    _____

Challenge

Write an essay explaining how John Howard Griffin's experiences proved that good or evil in human nature has nothing whatever to do with the color of a man or woman's skin.

Name _____   Date _____

A *Raisin in the Sun* by Lorraine Hansbury

Select the letter of the word or phrase which correctly completes each statement.

_____ 1. The set of the play is supposed to convey a sense of (A) shabbiness (B) over-crowdedness (C) exhaustion (D) all of the above.

_____ 2. The relationship between Ruth and Walter in the first scene may be best described as (A) indifference (B) hostility (C) loving frustration (D) sympathy.

_____ 3. All the characters in Act I are mainly interested in (A) Walter's job (B) Mama's insurance check (C) Travis' report card (D) Ruth's pregnancy.

_____ 4. Walter wants Ruth to (A) loan him some money (B) persuade Lena to give him money (C) be nicer to Beneatha (D) let Travis get an after-school job.

_____ 5. Lena (A) holds the family together (B) spoils Travis (C) doesn't understand the new ideas of the young (D) all of the above.

_____ 6. Beneatha doesn't really like George because he is (A) rich (B) poor (C) snobbish and shallow (D) uneducated.

_____ 7. The news of Ruth's pregnancy (A) makes Walter angry (B) is greeted joyously by everyone (C) makes Lena realize how desperate the situation is (D) is kept a secret.

_____ 8. Beneatha likes Asagai (A) because he understands her real needs (B) because he is African (C) because he brings her nice gifts (D) because he is studying medicine.

_____ 9. Walter feels that no one (A) listens to him (B) loves him (C) trusts him (D) thinks that he can be a success.

_____ 10. George Murchison insults Walter by (A) calling him "boy" (B) telling him he is a drunk (C) using language Walter doesn't understand (D) telling Walter he is stupid.

_____ 11. Mama first talks about the purchase of the house to (A) Ruth (B) Walter (C) Beneatha (D) Travis.

_____ 12. Ruth is concerned when she finds out that the house is (A) small (B) in a white neighborhood (C) too far from her work (D) owned by Lena.

_____ 13. Mama places her trust in Walter by (A) giving him the money to bank (B) putting him in charge of the movers (C) agreeing to meet Willie Harris (D) helping him find a new job.

_____ 14. Walter's dreams include (A) a fine car (B) a good school for Travis (C) a mansion (D) all of the above.

_____ 15. Karl Lindner (A) comes to welcome them to Claybourne Park (B) wants to buy the house back (C) threatens them cause Willie couldn't get the license.

_____ 17. The one who insists that they must move is (A) Mama (B) Ruth (C) Walter (D) Beneatha.

_____ 18. Originally, Walter intended to (A) accept Lindner's money (B) look for another job (C) move into the house anyway (D) go to Africa.

_____ 19. The person whose presence helps Walter stand up to Lindner is (A) Travis (B) Mama (C) Ruth (D) Asagai.

_____ 20. An important symbol for the family's survival is (A) Mama's hat (B) the plant (C) Ruth's ironing board (D) the insurance check.

©1986, 1991 J. Weston Walch, Publisher   *Great Books for Independent Reading*

Name _____ Date _____

A *Raisin in the Sun* by Lorraine Hansbury

Answer each of the following questions in two or three complete sentences.

1. What are some of the problems created by the Younger's crowded living situation?

    _____

    _____

    _____

    _____

2. Why does Beneatha like Asagai better than she likes George?

    _____

    _____

    _____

    _____

3. How does Lena show great courage and strength of character?

    _____

    _____

    _____

    _____

4. Despite their arguments, how does the play show that Walter and Ruth love each other?

    _____

    _____

    _____

    _____

5. How does Walter "come into his manhood" at the end of the play?

    _____

    _____

    _____

    _____

Challenge

The title of the play comes from Langston Hughes' poem, "A Dream Deferred." Read this short poem. Write an essay explaining how each of the attitudes expressed in the poem apply to characters in this play.

Name _____ Date _____

The Little Foxes by Lillian Hellman

Place a (+) before each statement that is true and a (0) before each statement that is false.

_____ 1. The dinner for Mr. Marshall takes place in Oscar and Birdie's home.

_____ 2. Birdie's family lost Lionnet because Birdie's brothers were too weak to hold on to it.

_____ 3. Alexandra is pleased with the idea of marrying Leo.

_____ 4. The Hubbards are planning a partnership with Marshall to build a cotton mill.

_____ 5. Regina wants to live in New York after the conclusion of the business deal.

_____ 6. Horace Giddens has cancer.

_____ 7. Birdie tries to warn Alexandra and to protect her from the Hubbards' scheming.

_____ 8. Regina forces Ben and Oscar to promise Horace fifty per cent of the mill profits.

_____ 9. When Horace returns home, he agrees at once to cooperate in the mill deal with Marshall.

_____ 10. Oscar Hubbard is pictured as a violent, vicious man.

_____ 11. Horace knows that Leo stole the bonds from the strongbox.

_____ 12. Birdie escapes from ugliness and unhappiness by drinking.

_____ 13. Horace does not want Alexandra to know about the evil and cruelty that exists within the family.

_____ 14. Horace intends to change his will to leave everything to Alexandra.

_____ 15. Horace collapses at the foot of the stairs.

_____ 16. Alexandra knows that her mother is at least partially responsible for her father's death.

_____ 17. Oscar sticks up for Leo when Leo is accused of theft.

_____ 18. Regina threatens to ruin her brothers if they do not give in to her demands for controlling interest in the mill.

_____ 19. Oscar suspects the truth about Regina's guilt in Horace's death.

_____ 20. In this play, the world seems to be controlled by those who are totally lacking in ethics and conscience.

Great Books for Independent Reading

Name _____ Date _____

The Little Foxes by Lillian Hellman

Answer each of the following questions in two or three complete sentences.

1. Contrast the personalities of Regina Giddens and Birdie Hubbard.

    _____

    _____

    _____

    _____

2. Why does Horace refuse to cooperate with the Hubbards in their business plans?

    _____

    _____

    _____

    _____

3. How does Regina show that she is just as ruthless as her brothers are?

    _____

    _____

    _____

    _____

4. In what ways is Alexandra more her father's daughter than her mother's daughter?

    _____

    _____

    _____

    _____

5. What evidences are there at the end of the play that Regina may have good reason to be afraid?

    _____

    _____

    _____

    _____

Challenge

The author divides the characters in *The Little Foxes* into three groups: those who eat the earth, those who fight, and those who stand around and watch. Write an essay, placing each of the play's characters into one of these three classifications. Which group seems to be victorious at the end?

Great Books for Independent Reading

Name _____   Date _____

Inherit the Wind by Jerome Lawrence and Robert E. Lee

Correctly complete each sentence with information from the play.

1. The atmosphere in Hillsboro before the trial may best be described as _____

   _____ .

2. Bertram Cates has been accused of _____ .

3. The chief attorney for the prosecution is _____ .

4. The attorney for the defense is _____ .

5. Hornbeck works for _____ .

6. Rachel wants Bert to _____ .

7. Brady's main character trait is his _____ .

8. When Melinda first sees Drummond, she thinks that he is _____ .

9. The court refuses to admit any of Drummond's evidence about _____ .

10. Drummond says that what is really on trial is _____ .

11. Rachel is very afraid of _____ .

12. Drummond calls as his witness for the defense _____ .

13. The jury finds Bert Cates _____ .

14. The judge sentences Bert _____ .

15. At the close of the trial, Brady intends to _____ .

16. Brady accuses Drummond of _____ .

17. When Brady starts to make his speech, the spectators _____ .

18. Cate's bail will be paid by _____ .

19. The judge comes back with the news that Brady _____ .

20. Rachel Brown has decided to _____ .

Name _____   Date _____

Inherit the Wind by Jerome Lawrence and Robert E. Lee

Answer each of the following questions in two or three complete sentences.

1. Why is the entire nation interested in the trial of Bert Cates?

_____

_____

_____

_____

2. Why is the atmosphere in Hillsboro prejudiced against Bert's getting a fair trial?

_____

_____

_____

_____

3. How is Rachel Brown trapped in the middle of the conflict?

_____

_____

_____

_____

4. How does Drummond trap Brady with Brady's own logic?

_____

_____

_____

_____

5. How does Drummond show respect for Brady as an opponent?

_____

_____

_____

_____

Challenge

Write an essay discussing how man's right to think is on trial in the case of Bertram Cates.

©1986, 1991 J. Weston Walch, Publisher

Great Books for Independent Reading

Name _____   Date _____

To Kill a Mockingbird by Harper Lee

Select the letter of the word or phrase which correctly completes each statement.

_____ 1. The story is told by (A) Jem (B) Scout (C) Atticus (D) Calpurnia.

_____ 2. Scout got into trouble her first day at school because of (A) Miss Caroline (B) Jem (C) Burris Ewell (D) Walter Cunningham.

_____ 3. Maycomb despised the Ewells because (A) they were crude (B) they were dirty (C) they lived in the town dump (D) all of the above.

_____ 4. The only "mother" that Scout could remember was (A) Aunt Alexandra (B) Calpurnia (C) Miss Maudie (D) Miss Caroline.

_____ 5. The children's imaginations were inspired by (A) Boo Radley (B) the arrival of Dill (C) the books they read (D) all of the above.

_____ 6. In escaping from the Radley house, Jem (A) was shot (B) lost his pants (C) actually saw Boo (D) stole some vegetables.

_____ 7. Boo Radley was (A) dangerous to the children (B) sociable (C) an adult with a child's mind (D) an only child.

_____ 8. Scout's favorite relative was (A) Uncle Jack (B) Cousin Francis (C) Aunt Alexandra (D) Uncle Jimmy.

_____ 9. Mrs. Dubose (A) had a nasty tongue (B) was a very sick old lady (C) helped Scout and Jem to learn patience (D) all of the above.

_____ 10. Tom Robinson was accused of (A) rape (B) murder (C) arson (D) larceny.

_____ 11. In defending Tom, Atticus had to face (A) the hatred of the Ewells (B) a lynch mob (C) the misunderstanding of the community (D) all of the above.

_____ 12. Atticus took Tom's case (A) because Tom was a friend of Calpurnia's (B) because Judge Taylor appointed him (C) because he thought that he could get Tom acquitted (D) because Atticus needed the publicity.

_____ 13. The children watched Tom's trial (A) through the window (B) from the front row (C) from the back of the courtroom (D) from the colored balcony.

_____ 14. Mayella Ewell (A) was trying to get even with Tom (B) was a victim of her father's cruelty and abuse (C) could speak clearly and logically (D) had actually been raped.

_____ 15. Tom could not have been Mayella's attacker (A) because he was a cripple (B) because he didn't enter the house (C) because he didn't know her (D) because he wasn't strong enough.

_____ 16. Tom was found guilty (A) because he was guilty (B) because he was black (C) because Atticus did a poor job defending him (D) because Bob Ewell's word was well-respected in the community.

_____ 17. Tom (A) was hanged (B) later went free (C) was shot trying to escape (D) was pardoned by Judge Taylor.

_____ 18. The injustice of the Robinson case was presented to the community by (A) Miss Maudie's letter to the paper (B) Mr. Underwood's editorial (C) Miss Gates' speech in class (D) Reverend Sykes' sermon.

_____ 19. On Halloween night, Scout's life was saved by (A) Jem (B) Atticus (C) Boo Radley (D) Sheriff Tate.

_____ 20. Bob Ewell died (A) when Jem stabbed him (B) when Boo stabbed him (C) when he fell on his own knife (D) when he was stabbed by the wires on Scout's costume.

©1986, 1991 J. Weston Walch, Publisher

Great Books for Independent Reading

Name _____ Date _____

To Kill a Mockingbird by Harper Lee

Answer each of the following questions in two or three complete sentences.

1. Why was Jem's and Scout's relationship with their father so special?

   _____

   _____

   _____

   _____

2. Why was school such a disaster for Scout?

   _____

   _____

   _____

   _____

3. What does Scout learn when she goes to church with Calpurnia?

   _____

   _____

   _____

   _____

4. Even though Atticus wishes to shield them, how do the children become involved in the events surrounding the Tom Robinson case?

   _____

   _____

   _____

   _____

5. Why does Mr. Underwood compare Tom's death to the killing of a mockingbird?

   _____

   _____

   _____

   _____

Challenge

In what ways would the childhood experiences recounted in *To Kill a Mockingbird* help Jean Louise Finch to grow into a compassionate, less prejudiced adult?

Name _____ Date _____

Main Street by Sinclair Lewis

Select the letter of the word or phrase which correctly completes each statement.

_____ 1. Carol met and married Will Kennicott when she was (A) a teenager (B) a college student (C) a young librarian (D) an office worker in Washington.

_____ 2. Carol's idealism became focused on (A) slum clearance (B) small-town reform (C) education (D) temperance.

_____ 3. After she had been in Gopher Prairie for a few months, Carol's main feeling was (A) entrapment (B) indifference (C) anger (D) enjoyment.

_____ 4. The person whose initial reaction to Gopher Prairie was most opposite to Carol's was (A) Erik's (B) Bea Sorenson (C) Sam Clark (D) Fern Mullins.

_____ 5. Carol realizes that the town accepts her only because (A) her husband is one of them (B) she is a college student (C) she is young and intelligent (D) they agree with her ideas about small-town reform.

_____ 6. Kennicott's interests included all of the following except (A) automobiles (B) agriculture (C) land speculation (D) hunting.

_____ 7. Carol's closest female friend in Gopher Prairie was (A) Maud Dyer (B) Mrs. Bogart (C) Vida Sherwin (D) Juanita Haycock.

_____ 8. Carol's first party was seen by the town as (A) overdone (B) pretentious (C) Carol's attempt to show off (D) all of the above.

_____ 9. The most ironic name that Lewis uses for a town organization is (A) Thanatopsis (B) Jolly Seventeen (C) Bon-Ton (D) Gopher Prairie Drama Society.

_____ 10. Carol tries to improve all of the following except (A) the Baptist Church (B) the town hall (C) the school (D) the library.

_____ 11. The dullness of small-town life is also understood by (A) Kennicott (B) Guy Pollock (C) Sam Clark (D) Mrs. Champ Clark.

_____ 12. Victims of Gopher Prairie's prejudices include all of the following except: (A) Maud Dyer (B) Miles Bjornstam (C) Bea Soronson (D) Fern Mullins.

_____ 13. Erik's father blames his son's problems on (A) the Jolly Seventeen (B) Carol (C) Erik's employer (D) Dr. Kennicott.

_____ 14. The most vicious hypocrite in the town is (A) Vida Sherwin (B) Aunt Bessie (C) Mrs. Bogart (D) Mrs. Champ Clark.

_____ 15. Carol is drawn to Eric because she feels that they are both (A) sensitive (B) artistic (C) outcasts (D) intelligent.

_____ 16. The most positive element in Carol's life is (A) her husband (B) her son (C) the Jolly Seventeen (D) Thanatopsis.

_____ 17. Carol and Kennicott have their most serious quarrel over (A) Erik (B) Fern Mullins (C) building a new home (D) Harry Blausser's improvement campaign.

_____ 18. Carol finds her desire for a larger world in (A) New York (B) Washington (C) Minneapolis (D) Los Angeles.

_____ 19. When Kennicott comes to visit Carol, he (A) courts and woos her (B) demands that she return home (C) makes fun of her work (D) asks her for a divorce.

_____ 20. At the end of the novel, Carol sees the continuation of her hopes in (A) her children (B) the new school building (C) the new library (D) the revival of her love for Kennicott.

Name _____ Date _____

Main Street by Sinclair Lewis

Answer each of the following questions in two or three complete sentences.

1. What dreams does Carol have for Gopher Prairie? How are these dreams reduced to frustrations during the first years of her marriage?

   _____

   _____

   _____

   _____

2. How is the marriage of Bea and Miles more real than the marriage of Carol and Kennicott?

   _____

   _____

   _____

   _____

3. Why is Carol's attraction to Erik destined to produce heartbreak?

   _____

   _____

   _____

   _____

4. What is the "Village Virus"? Why is it so deadly to Carol Kennicott?

   _____

   _____

   _____

   _____

5. How does Fern Mullins become a victim of everything that is evil in Gopher Prairie?

   _____

   _____

   _____

   _____

Challenge

Write an essay discussing the character development of Carol Kennicott. How does she change from a starry-eyed idealist to a mature woman who can cope with reality? What are some of the experiences which produce these changes?

Great Books for Independent Reading

Name _____   Date _____

The Crucible by Arthur Miller

Correctly complete each sentence with information from the play.

1. Parris had frequent conflicts with his congregation about _____.

2. _____ had learned the techniques of witchcraft on the island of _____.

3. Abigail and the girls had been caught by Parris when they were _____.

4. Elizabeth Proctor had fired Abigail because _____.

5. The character who best presents the voice of common sense in the rising hysterics is _____.

6. Thomas Putnam's enemies in his land disputes were _____ and _____.

7. Parris has sent for Reverend Hale because _____.

8. Ruth Putnam accuses Rebecca Nurse of _____.

9. The relationship between John and Elizabeth Proctor at the beginning of Act II may best be described as _____.

10. Mary Warren is afraid of Abigail because _____.

11. When Hale asks Proctor to repeat the commandments, the one that John misses is _____.

12. Elizabeth knows that Abigail has accused her of witchcraft so that _____.

13. Giles Corey and Francis Nurse try to save their wives by _____.

14. _____ is the chief justice of the court.

15. When Mary Warren tries to tell the truth, Abigail _____.

16. Hale quits the court because _____.

17. Hale tries to get Rebecca and John to confess so that _____.

18. Elizabeth's life is saved because _____.

19. Giles Corey dies by _____ because he will not _____.

20. John will not sign the confession because _____.

Name _____ Date _____

The Crucible by Arthur Miller

Explain in two or three sentences the meaning of each of the following quotes or character descriptions.

1. "He have his goodness now. God forbid that I should take it from him."

   _____

   _____

   _____

   _____

2. "A strikingly beautiful girl with an endless capacity for dissembling."

   _____

   _____

   _____

   _____

3. "Elizabeth, your justice would freeze beer."

   _____

   _____

   _____

   _____

4. "We are only what we always were, but naked now . . . and God's icy wind will blow."

   _____

   _____

   _____

   _____

5. "In his presence, a fool felt his foolishness instantly."

   _____

   _____

   _____

   _____

Challenge

The Salem witchcraft trials resulted in the destruction of a society. Describe the roots of hate, jealousy, and greed which were the real forces behind the hysterics. Discuss the characters which best illustrate these attitudes.

Great Books for Independent Reading

Name _____ Date _____

Animal Farm by George Orwell

Place a (+) before each statement that is true and a (0) before each statement that is false.

_____   1.   Snowball had the dream which envisioned the ideal animal society.

_____   2.   Jones was a cruel farmer who abused and neglected his animals.

_____   3.   The basic principle of the revolution at the beginning was that some animals were superior to other animals.

_____   4.   Major led the battle to drive Jones and his men from the farm.

_____   5.   Snowball was a better speaker and organizer than Napoleon was.

_____   6.   Education was an important part of the animals' revolutionary program.

_____   7.   Napoleon favored the building of the windmill, while Snowball opposed it.

_____   8.   Snowball returned to Animal Farm several times after Napoleon's dogs drove him off.

_____   9.   Benjamin was the perfect example of the hard worker who believed everything that he was told.

_____ 10.   The animals successfully defended the farm at the Battle of the Cowshed.

_____ 11.   Clover was lured away from Animal Farm by her love of sugar and bright ribbons.

_____ 12.   Squealer was responsible for changing the Animal Commandments to justify everything that the pigs did.

_____ 13.   Napoleon himself took the responsibility for the accidental destruction of the first windmill.

_____ 14.   Napoleon used Mr. Pilkington as an agent to trade for the necessities that Animal Farm could not produce.

_____ 15.   As time passed, the lifestyle of the average animal improved substantially.

_____ 16.   All errors and problems were blamed on Snowball.

_____ 17.   Napoleon and his pigs continued to encourage the other animals by frequently singing "Beasts of England."

_____ 18.   All the animals were allowed to drink some of the whiskey that was produced on the farm.

_____ 19.   No animals ever challenged Napoleon's authority.

_____ 20.   Boxer was the animal who was most betrayed by the revolution he had believed in.

Name _____   Date _____

Animal Farm by George Orwell

Answer each of the following questions in two or three complete sentences.

1. Describe the animals' utopian vision of an ideal society.

    _____

    _____

    _____

    _____

2. How did Napoleon gain absolute control of Animal Farm?

    _____

    _____

    _____

    _____

3. In what specific ways was Squealer valuable as a propaganda expert?

    _____

    _____

    _____

    _____

4. How did life on Animal Farm gradually change for the average animal?

    _____

    _____

    _____

    _____

5. How did the pigs finally become just like the men they had driven out?

    _____

    _____

    _____

    _____

Challenge

Write an essay discussing Orwell's use of personification. How do the characteristics of the various animals represent traits evident in human nature?

Name _____ Date _____

Cry, the Beloved Country by Alan Paton

In the numbered blanks at the left, write the letter of the matching person or place.

_____ 1. Stephen's guide and closest friend in Johannesburg

_____ 2. Skilled speaker who had been corrupted by his love for power

_____ 3. God

_____ 4. Kumalo's home village

_____ 5. Struck Jarvis's houseboy on the head with a crowbar

_____ 6. Organizer of the bus boycott to protest a rate increase

_____ 7. Said that he fired his gun because he was afraid

_____ 8. Reverend, pastor

_____ 9. Brought up Gertrude's child as her own son

_____ 10. English priest who married the girl to Absalom

_____ 11. Planned to build a new church for the people of the village

_____ 12. Jarvis's brother-in-law whose opinions represent the views of the South African white community

_____ 13. Returned to a life of crime and prostitution

_____ 14. Stephen's tribe

_____ 15. Came to the valley to teach scientific farming methods

_____ 16. Title of respect used by the blacks for a white man

_____ 17. Gave Stephen and Gertrude a place to live in Johannesburg

_____ 18. Powerful writer who believed that South Africa must recognize the humanity of her black population

_____ 19. Absalom's landlady

_____ 20. Lawyer for the defense

A. Umfundisi
B. Umnumzana
C. John Kumalo
D. Johannes Pafuri
E. Gertrude
F. Mr. Carmichael
G. Father Vincent
H. John Harrison
I. Arthur Jarvis
J. Ndotsheni
K. James Jarvis
L. Msimangu
M. Mrs. Mkize
N. Absalom
O. Mrs. Lithebe
P. Zulu
Q. Tixo
R. Napoleon Letsitsi
S. Mrs. Kumalo
T. Dubula

Name _____   Date _____

Cry, the Beloved Country by Alan Paton

Answer each of the following questions in two or three complete sentences.

1. Describe Kumalo's initial reactions when he arrives in Johannesburg.

    _____

    _____

    _____

    _____

2. Contrast Stephen Kumalo and his brother John.

    _____

    _____

    _____

    _____

3. How does Stephen's family represent the breakdown of the South African tribal system?

    _____

    _____

    _____

    _____

4. How do Msimangu and Mrs. Lithebe represent goodness and humanity against a background of injustice and evil?

    _____

    _____

    _____

    _____

5. How are both Absalom Kumalo and Arthur Jarvis victims of the social evils of South Africa?

    _____

    _____

    _____

    _____

Challenge

Write an essay describing the hopes which Alan Paton has for his country. Where does Paton believe that the fulfillment of these hopes lies?

©1986, 1991 J. Weston Walch, Publisher

Great Books for Independent Reading

Name _____   Date _____

Twelve Angry Men by Reginald Rose

In the numbered blanks at the left, write the letter of the matching person or place. Some letters may be used more than once.

_____	1.	Was himself the product of a slum environment
_____	2.	Charged the jury that their vote had to be unanimous
_____	3.	Eyesight was called into question
_____	4.	Insists from the beginning that the jury members take some time to give the case a fair hearing
_____	5.	Wanted to get done quickly so he could get to a baseball game
_____	6.	Inexperienced and lax, appointed by the court
_____	7.	Setting for most of the play
_____	8.	Verified from his experience that the old man could not have heard the body fall because of the noise from the train
_____	9.	The most violent member of the group, capable of being a killer himself
_____	10.	Man of weak opinions, changed his vote twice because he was easily swayed by the others
_____	11.	Oldest member of the jury, identified with the old man's need for respect and attention
_____	12.	Most cultured of the jury members
_____	13.	Had been declared by a psychiatrist as being capable of killing
_____	14.	Could not have moved fast enough to see the boy run away
_____	15.	Bigot, who saw the boy as one of "them"
_____	16.	Timed the reenactment of the old man's walk to the hall
_____	17.	An immigrant who took his responsibilities to democracy very seriously
_____	18.	Tried to keep the tempers of the others under control
_____	19.	Brought in the pieces of evidence for examination
_____	20.	Violent man who had served a term in prison

A. #8
B. The old man
C. The boy's lawyer
D. The boy's father
E. #3
F. #7
G. #10
H. #4
I. The foreman
J. #5
K. #11
L. #6
M. #9
N. Woman witness
O. Guard
P. #12
Q. #2
R. The judge
S. The defendant
T. The jury room

Great Books for Independent Reading

Name _____ Date _____

Twelve Angry Men by Reginald Rose

Answer each of the following questions in two or three complete sentences.

1. Why does #8 vote "not guilty" on the first ballot?

   _____

   _____

   _____

   _____

2. How does the attitude of #8 toward the boy and the crime contrast with the attitude of #10?

   _____

   _____

   _____

   _____

3. Why does #5 understand, better than any of the others, the feelings of the defendant?

   _____

   _____

   _____

   _____

4. Why does the author of the play give the jury members numbers instead of names?

   _____

   _____

   _____

   _____

5. Why is #7 really the weakest of the jury members when the final vote comes?

   _____

   _____

   _____

   _____

Challenge

The true nature of a person's character emerges when that person is subjected to stress and pressure. Select three of the jurors and describe how true character comes out in the pressure of the jury room.

Great Books for Independent Reading

Name _____ Date _____

A *Majority of One* by Leonard Spigelgass

Correctly complete each sentence with information from the play.

1. Jerry Black works for _____.

2. Jerry and Alice have just received a transfer to _____.

3. Essie Rubin is concerned about the quality of her neighborhood because _____
   _____.

4. Mrs. Jacoby has strong feelings against the Japanese because _____
   _____.

5. Jerry and Alice want Mrs. Jacoby to _____
   _____.

6. When Mrs. Jacoby first meets Mr. Asano, she _____.

7. Mr. Asano tells Mrs. Jacoby that his son and daughter _____
   _____.

8. Jerry is concerned about Mrs. Jacoby's friendship with Mr. Asano because _____
   _____.

9. Eddie, the Japanese houseboy, says that he is losing face because _____
   _____.

10. As a girl, Mrs. Jacoby had come to America from _____.

11. Jerry is upset because the trade negotiations have _____.

12. Mrs. Jacoby decides to help Jerry by _____.

13. Mrs. Jacoby tells Mr. Asano that his company needs to _____.

14. Alice and Jerry have called the military police to _____.

15. Among the gifts that Mr. Asano gives Mrs. Jacoby are _____

    and _____.

16. Mr. Asano asks Mrs. Jacoby to _____.

17. Mrs. Jacoby refuses because _____.

18. Mrs. Jacoby decides that she wishes to _____.

19. In the concluding scene of the play, Mr. Asano _____.

20. Mrs. Jacoby and Mr. Asano decide to _____.

Great Books for Independent Reading

Name _____ Date _____

A *Majority of One* by Leonard Spigelgass

Answer each of the following questions in two or three complete sentences.

1. How does Mrs. Jacoby illustrate her motherly instincts on the sea voyage?

    _____

    _____

    _____

    _____

2. Why do Jerry and Alice insist that Mrs. Jacoby accompany them?

    _____

    _____

    _____

    _____

3. What danger of the diplomatic service is Mrs. Jacoby warned about?

    _____

    _____

    _____

    _____

4. What does Mrs. Jacoby's dinner with Mr. Asano accomplish?

    _____

    _____

    _____

    _____

5. Why can Mrs. Jacoby and Mr. Asano be friends in New York easier than they could be in Japan?

    _____

    _____

    _____

    _____

Challenge

Write an essay showing how the plot of this play illustrates Jerry Black's statement: "If you want to stop prejudice, you've got to stop it in yourself" (p. 124).

Great Books for Independent Reading

Name _____   Date _____

The Hiding Place by Corrie Ten Boom

In the numbered blanks at the left, write the letter of the matching person or place.

_____ 1. Organization of Dutchmen who collaborated with the Germans

_____ 2. German officer who arranged a reunion for the family in an Amsterdam prison

_____ 3. Where Corrie grew up

_____ 4. Helped supply the underground with hundreds of needed ration cards

_____ 5. Was imprisoned for playing the Dutch national anthem

_____ 6. German death camp where Betsie died

_____ 7. Holland's first licensed woman watchmaker

_____ 8. Prisoner-foreman in the radio factory

_____ 9. Strange-shaped old house where refugees could be hidden

_____ 10. Prison hospital worker who got the women medicine and vitamins

_____ 11. Dutch policeman who helped the underground

_____ 12. Means "Grandfather," children's nickname for Corrie's father

_____ 13. Code name used by the underground to protect each person's identity

_____ 14. Relative who wrote tracts and was a champion of various social causes

_____ 15. Sister with a special kind of love, even for their German captors

_____ 16. Man that Corrie loved

_____ 17. Managed to smuggle in a blue sweater to keep Betsie warm

_____ 18. Nickname for the man who became the head of the underground operation

_____ 19. Corrie's brother, an ordained minister

_____ 20. Old watchmaker who was persecuted by the young German, Otto

A. Beje
B. Haarlem
C. Tante Jans
D. Opa
E. Christoffels
F. Peter
G. Wilhelm
H. Betsie
I. Nollie
J. Corrie
K. Karel
L. NSB
M. Fred Koornstra
N. Rolf
O. "Pickwick"
P. Mr. Smit
Q. Ravensbruck
R. Mien
S. Mr. Mooman
T. Lieutenant Rahms

Name _____   Date _____

The Hiding Place by Corrie Ten Boom

Answer each of the following questions in two or three complete sentences.

1. How was Corrie's father a great influence in the community?

   _____

   _____

   _____

   _____

2. How was Corrie's disposition different from Betsie's?

   _____

   _____

   _____

   _____

3. What methods did the Ten Booms use to hide and protect their Jewish friends?

   _____

   _____

   _____

   _____

4. What examples of human kindness did Corrie find, even in the horror of the prisons and the concentration camp?

   _____

   _____

   _____

   _____

5. What kind of new work did Corrie begin after her release from prison?

   _____

   _____

   _____

   _____

Challenge

Corrie Ten Boom believes that the strength to survive will be given as that strength is needed. Write an essay giving some examples from her experiences which prove this statement to be true.

Great Books for Independent Reading

Name _____ Date _____

Native Son by Richard Wright

In the numbered blanks at the left, write the letter of the matching person.

_____ 1. Entered Mary's room and smelled the liquor

_____ 2. Found escape and consolation in her religion

_____ 3. Police officer who was injured by Bigger in his attempt to evade capture

_____ 4. Delivered Mary's trunk to the railroad station

_____ 5. Used the publicity of Bigger's trial to advantage in a campaign for reelection

_____ 6. Owned the tenement building in which Bigger and his family lived

_____ 7. Black minister who tried to help Bigger

_____ 8. Bigger's younger sister

_____ 9. Friend who shared Bigger's movie fantasies

_____ 10. Wore valuable earrings that were inherited from her grandmother

_____ 11. Murdered by Bigger because she endangered his escape

_____ 12. White delicatessen owner whom the boys intended to rob

_____ 13. Treated Bigger as an equal by shaking hands with him

_____ 14. One of the men who discovered Mary's body in the furnace

_____ 15. Pled with the court to spare Bigger's life because Bigger was himself a victim

_____ 16. Witnessed Bigger's disposal of Mary's body

_____ 17. Private investigator employed by Mary's father

_____ 18. Was attacked by Bigger because he sensed Bigger's fear

_____ 19. Dalton housekeeper who was kind to Bigger

_____ 20. Helped Bigger kill a large black rat

A. White Cat
B. Mrs. Thomas
C. Buddy
D. Mr. Blum
E. Vera
F. Peggy
G. Mr. Dalton
H. Gus
I. Mrs. Dalton
J. Jan
K. Mary
L. Britten
M. Bigger
N. Toorman
O. Hammond
P. Max
Q. Buckley
R. Bessie
S. Jack
T. Jerry

Name _____   Date _____

Native Son by Richard Wright

Answer each of the following questions in two or three complete sentences.

1. What were some causes of Bigger's feelings of frustration?

    _____

    _____

    _____

    _____

2. In what ways was Mary Dalton's death an accident?

    _____

    _____

    _____

    _____

3. Why was Jan's and Mary's behavior toward him very confusing to Bigger?

    _____

    _____

    _____

    _____

4. How did the police finally capture Bigger?

    _____

    _____

    _____

    _____

5. Why did Buckley insist that Bigger must die for his crimes?

    _____

    _____

    _____

    _____

Challenge

Write an essay summarizing Max's arguments, which represent Richard Wright's philosophy, that society itself is responsible for the crimes of Bigger Thomas.

Great Books for Independent Reading

Answer Keys

To Sir With Love by E.R. Braithwaite

OBJECTIVE:

1. J	6. A	11. N
2. C	7. D	12. E
3. O	8. K	13. M
4. F	9. G	14. I
5. L	10. B	15. H

SHORT ANSWER:

1. Couldn't find a job as an engineer—was rejected because he was black. Prejudice was always hidden.
2. Broken homes, had to work at a very young age, grew up fighting for survival.
3. To bring order to the class, to teach them respect for others.
4. Interest in customs and cultures of other countries, museums, music, ballet.
5. Grows from a girl into a woman, new understanding of her mother's situation, willing to defy prejudice to take flowers to the black family.

CHALLENGE:

Students learn to be ladies and gentlemen. Learn the realities of a world outside their own. "Sir" learns to understand their view of life, to receive their love and affection.

The Good Earth by Pearl S. Buck

OBJECTIVE:

1. C	6. B	11. C	16. B
2. D	7. C	12. C	17. A
3. B	8. B	13. A	18. C
4. D	9. D	14. D	19. C
5. A	10. B	15. C	20. C

SHORT ANSWER:

1. Plows the earth with him, looks after his aged father, helps the family survive the flood, keeps the family together in the city so they can return to the land.
2. Land is the link with the past and the hope for the future.
3. Love of shared experience versus physical infatuation.
4. Dictates what his sons must do, gives them no choice, fails to educate them in the traditional values.
5. Corrupted by wealth and luxury, removal from the land to the city, total loss of the old ways.

CHALLENGE:

Novel chronicles the destruction of the Oriental family ideals. Wang deserts O-lan for Lotus. Sons become alienated from the father. The uncle and his son join the robbers. After Wang's death the sons will take over and the land will be gone.

ANSWER KEYS (continued)

The Chocolate War by Robert Cormier

OBJECTIVE:

1. I	6. N	11. B	16. N
2. M	7. L	12. J	17. J
3. O	8. C	13. G	18. D
4. H	9. E	14. A	19. M
5. F	10. K	15. D	20. O

SHORT ANSWER:

1. Becomes his act of individual defiance against the system.
2. Leon's main desire for control. Plans to use the Vigils as a tool to exercise this control.
3. If the leader draws the black spot, he must complete the assignment.
4. Obscene phone calls, destruction of the poster in his locker, art project gets "lost."
5. Boys gang up to fight Jerry. He is brutally beaten. Brother Jacques turns out the lights.

CHALLENGE:

Theme of the book is individual rights against a corrupt system. Even though he is beaten by overwhelming odds, Jerry gains nobility by his refusal to give in. Jerry's strength in opposition to the weaker boys who allow themselves to be controlled.

I Am the Cheese by Robert Cormier

OBJECTIVE:

1. 0	6. +	11. 0	16. 0
2. +	7. 0	12. 0	17. +
3. 0	8. +	13. 0	18. 0
4. +	9. +	14. 0	19. 0
5. 0	10. 0	15. +	20. 0

SHORT ANSWER:

1. He saves his package, he fights to get his bike back.
2. He relaxes with her and talks about himself. He has fun in her "capers."
3. His father testified against organized crime.
4. Two birth certificates, the editor who does not know his family, the aunt that he didn't know he had.
5. Her fears for their future. Never knowing when Mr. Gray would tell them to move again.

CHALLENGE:

Phrase from "Farmer in the Dell," "the cheese stands alone." Must fight Brint, the drugs, the system which wants to destroy him. Perhaps he can't survive, but he will fight to the end, just like he continued to struggle on his bike trip.

The Autobiography of Miss Jane Pittman by Ernest J. Gaines

OBJECTIVE:

1. +	6. +	11. 0	16. 0
2. 0	7. +	12. +	17. 0
3. 0	8. +	13. +	18. 0
4. 0	9. 0	14. 0	19. 0
5. 0	10. +	15. 0	20. +

ANSWER KEYS (continued)

The Autobiography of Miss Jane Pittman by Ernest J. Gaines (continued)

SHORT ANSWER:

1. Ate stolen potatoes and corn, kept hidden from gangs of killers, followed the river.
2. Made them sign papers that they couldn't read, kept them on plantations doing menial jobs and living in terrible conditions.
3. To educate the blacks, to better their lives.
4. A white man couldn't marry a black, but could keep her as his mistress. Robert really loved Mary Agnes. Suicide was the only way out.
5. The deliverer who could provide the leadership for real social change.

CHALLENGE:

Maintained her pride, even when she was a slave. Fought to keep Ned and herself alive. Rose to the position of trusted servant to the Samson family. In her old age, she was willing to participate in the civil rights struggle.

Black Like Me by John Howard Griffin

OBJECTIVE:

1. a journalist
2. his skin color
3. New Orleans
4. medication and sunlamp treatments
5. Sterling Williams
6. looking in the mirror
7. restrooms, drinking fountains
8. economic advancement
9. Parker
10. the look whites gave blacks
11. those with the lightest skin
12. P.D. East
13. Negro's sex life
14. shared the cabin with the black family
15. Montgomery, Alabama
16. *Sepia*
17. loneliness
18. six months
19. burned him in effigy
20. move somewhere else

SHORT ANSWER:

1. Medication from a dermatologist, sunlamp treatments, dye to darken the area around his face and eyes.
2. To find out how being black really felt.
3. New Orleans—ignored or politely put in his place. Mississippi—treated like an animal or a curiosity.
4. Family had to leave town. Articles received well by some, but attracted the fury of the southern whites.
5. That the Negroes will become as angry and as racist as the whites are.

CHALLENGE:

Good whites—P.D. East, the girl in the bookstore, the monks. Good blacks—the family who took him in, Sterling Williams, the shoeshine man. Bad whites—the bus driver, the lady ticket seller, the sexually curious. Bad blacks—Christophe, the man on the bus. The only way that Griffin was any different was in his skin color. Not his morals, manners, or education.

A Raisin in the Sun by Lorraine Hansbury

OBJECTIVE:

1. D	6. C	11. D	16. A
2. C	7. C	12. B	17. B
3. B	8. A	13. A	18. A
4. B	9. A	14. D	19. A
5. D	10. C	15. B	20. B

ANSWER KEYS (continued)

A Raisin in the Sun by Lorraine Hansbury (continued)

SHORT ANSWER:

1. No privacy, everything shabby, no room for Travis to sleep, emotional pressures of overcrowding.
2. Asagai—genuine and caring. George is a fake and a snob.
3. Buys a house in the white neighborhood. Tries to keep the family together.
4. Each wants the best for the other. Ruth feels the helplessness of Walter's frustration— Walter wants to fulfill his great dreams for his family.
5. He defies Lindner and says that the family will move into their house.

CHALLENGE:

The failure of old Walter's hopes—the dream which dries up. Festering—Beneathea's anger. Stinking—fakeness of George. Crusting over—Lena's feelings of failure. Heavy load—reaction to Ruth's pregnancy. Explode—Walter's blowup at George.

The Little Foxes by Lillian Hellman

OBJECTIVE:

1. 0	6. 0	11. +	16. +
2. +	7. +	12. +	17. 0
3. 0	8. 0	13. 0	18. +
4. +	9. 0	14. 0	19. 0
5. 0	10. +	15. 0	20. +

SHORT ANSWER:

1. Regina—dominating and vicious. Birdie—dependent and victimized.
2. He will not participate in their destructive greed.
3. She allows Horace to die so she can have her way.
4. She is caring, has a sense of morality.
5. Oscar suspects the truth about Horace's death.

CHALLENGE:

The Hubbards and Regina are the eaters. Horace and Alexandra are the fighters. Birdie stands helplessly and watches.

Inherit the Wind by Jerome Lawrence and Robert E. Lee

OBJECTIVE:

1.	a carnival	7.	egotism	13.	guilty	17.	leave
2.	teaching evolution	8.	the devil	14.	$100 fine	18.	Hornbeck's
3.	Brady	9.	scientific theory	15.	make a speech		newspaper
4.	Drummond	10.	the right to think	16.	destroying	19.	is dead
5.	*Baltimore Sun*	11.	her father		people's faith	20.	leave her father
6.	give up and quit	12.	Brady				and go with Bert

SHORT ANSWER:

1. Drama of the confrontation between Brady and Drummond.
2. Bible-preaching forces controlled the town. No room for any dissenting opinion.
3. Caught between her loyalty to her father and her love for Bert.
4. Tricks Brady into admitting that perhaps the Bible might not be the only authority.
5. Eulogizes Brady's lost greatness—scene of weighing the copy of the Bible with the copy of Darwin.

ANSWER KEYS (continued)

Inherit the Wind by Jerome Lawrence and Robert E. Lee (continued)

CHALLENGE:

Play presents the right to think about alternatives. The open mind of Bert opposed to the closed attitude of the community. Desmond's triumph—the right to think. Brady's tragedy—the brilliant speaker but the closed mind.

To Kill a Mockingbird by Harper Lee

OBJECTIVE:

1. B	6. B	11. D	16. B
2. D	7. C	12. B	17. C
3. D	8. A	13. D	18. B
4. B	9. D	14. B	19. C
5. D	10. A	15. A	20. B

SHORT ANSWER:

1. Talks to them on adult level, answers their questions, reads to them and makes time for them.
2. Tries to explain about the Cunninghams, gets into trouble because she can read and write. Generally bored with the whole thing.
3. That Calpurnia is different with the blacks, that race prejudice exists on both sides.
4. Kids get called names and get into fights at school, watch the trial from the colored balcony.
5. Senseless destruction of that which is innocent.

CHALLENGE:

Tom Robinson case, learning to see the reality of prejudice. Courage from Mrs. Dubose. At the missionary society—how to keep her head in time of crisis. Not to believe hearsay, to understand the other person's situation—Boo Radley.

Main Street by Sinclair Lewis

OBJECTIVE:

1. C	6. B	11. B	16. B
2. B	7. C	12. A	17. D
3. A	8. D	13. B	18. B
4. B	9. B	14. C	19. A
5. A	10. A	15. C	20. A

SHORT ANSWER:

1. To make Gopher Prairie a model small town. They are satisfied with the status quo.
2. They share a life and love and care for each other.
3. Erik has the gentleness and sensitivity that Will lacks.
4. The entrapment of the small town. The mind and the spirit will die.
5. She is driven out. Her life is destroyed by the evil minds and vicious tongues.

CHALLENGE:

Begins with high ideals, but is disillusioned by experience. Tries to make a difference and fails. Rejects Erik's love—escapes to Washington. Returns to life with Will. Sees hope for a difference in her children.

ANSWER KEYS (continued)

The Crucible by Arthur Miller

OBJECTIVE:

1. his salary, the deed to his house
2. Tituba, Barbados
3. dancing naked in the woods
4. Elizabeth knew of Abigail's affair with John
5. Rebecca Nurse
6. Francis Nurse, Giles Corey
7. he was a witch-craft expert
8. killing her children
9. cold, suspicious
10. Abigail threatens her
11. adultery
12. Abigail can have John
13. bringing a petition to the court
14. Danforth
15. turns and accuses her
16. the whole thing has gone out of control
17. their lives can be saved
18. she is pregnant
19. being crushed, confess
20. he wants to keep his name

SHORT ANSWER:

1. Proctor found nobility and a freedom from guilt through death.
2. Abigail could totally change her personality to fit any situation.
3. Elizabeth never really forgave John.
4. The real motives for people's behavior would come out.
5. Proctor made others uncomfortable because he could see through their actions.

CHALLENGE:

Putnam's hatred for Nurse over church fight. Putnam greed for land. Abigail's jealousy and desire for John, desire for revenge against Elizabeth. Parris' paranoia.

Animal Farm by George Orwell

OBJECTIVE:

1. 0	6. +	11. 0	16. +
2. +	7. 0	12. +	17. 0
3. 0	8. 0	13. 0	18. 0
4. 0	9. 0	14. 0	19. 0
5. +	10. +	15. 0	20. +

SHORT ANSWER:

1. Society where all animals would be equal and all would receive the reward for their work.
2. Destroyed the plans for the windmill, drove out Snowball, used the dogs to keep control.
3. Changed all of the commandments and rules to fit what Napoleon wanted.
4. Became much worse—harder work, fewer benefits for the masses, privilege to pigs alone.
5. Lived in the house, drank liquor, used whips to keep the others in line.

CHALLENGE:

Lust for power—Napoleon. Unquestioning loyalty—Boxer. Opportunist—Squealer. Vanity—Molly. Entire book is an allegory to illustrate how the communist revolution failed. Average life was worse—new ruling class replaced the old.

ANSWER KEYS (continued)

Cry, the Beloved Country by Alan Paton

OBJECTIVE:

1. L	6. T	11. I	16. B
2. C	7. N	12. H	17. O
3. Q	8. A	13. E	18. I
4. J	9. S	14. P	19. M
5. D	10. G	15. R	20. F

SHORT ANSWER:

1. Confusion at the size and noise, grief for what the city has done to his family.
2. Stephen faithful to God and traditional values. John a political opportunist with no morals left.
3. Lured to the city and into crime for money. Controlled by fear. Old ways gone with nothing to replace them.
4. Msimangu—helped Stephen find his son. Lawyer took Absalom's case free. Mrs. Lithebe tried to help Gertrude and the girl.
5. Absalom victim of the white man's greed destroying the society. Arthur killed by one of the blacks that he wished to help.

CHALLENGE:

Restoration of the land and the tribe. Meaning for the individual life in spiritual values. Hope in understanding, in the new generation like Arthur Jarvis' son.

Twelve Angry Men by Reginald Rose

OBJECTIVE:

1. J	6. C	11. M	16. Q
2. R	7. T	12. H	17. K
3. N	8. L	13. S	18. I
4. A	9. E	14. B	19. O
5. F	10. P	15. M	20. D

SHORT ANSWER:

1. He feels that they should at least discuss the case.
2. #8 remains openminded. #10 is sure that the boy is guilty.
3. He came from the same kind of background.
4. They represent a typical cross-section of human attitudes.
5. He changes his vote just to get the whole thing over with—no convictions.

CHALLENGE:

#3 hatred for his own son comes out, and his violence as he attacks #8. #10 total bigot—hatred for "those kind of people." #9 little man who has always been ignored—identified with the man who testifies to get attention. #11 sensitive because he was a refugee.

ANSWER KEYS (continued)

A Majority of One by Leonard Spigelgass

OBJECTIVE:

1. U.S. State Department
2. Japan
3. blacks and Puerto Ricans are moving in
4. her son was killed in the war
5. go to Japan
6. snubs him
7. were killed by the American forces
8. Asano will use that friendship in the negotiations
9. Mrs. Jacoby does all the work
10. Russia
11. totally broken off
12. going to see Mr. Asano
13. diversify
14. find Mrs. Jacoby
15. kimono, a set of china
16. keep company with him
17. thinks too much of Sam
18. go home to New York
19. has dinner with Mrs. Jacoby
20. be friends and enjoy each other's company

SHORT ANSWER:

1. Concern for Mr. Asano's health, for everyone's welfare.
2. So they can look after her.
3. Being offered friendship by people who want favors in return.
4. Gets him to compromise and reopen the talks.
5. Their friendship will not be bound by Japanese custom or linked to Jerry's job.

CHALLENGE:

Mrs. Jacoby and Mr. Asano are both able to see each other as individuals, not as members of nations in the war. Jerry learns of his own prejudices created by his job.

The Hiding Place by Corrie Ten Boom

OBJECTIVE:

1. L
2. T
3. B
4. M
5. F
6. Q
7. J
8. S
9. A
10. R
11. N
12. D
13. P
14. C
15. H
16. K
17. I
18. O
19. G
20. E

SHORT ANSWER:

1. He shared his faith with his neighbors, loved children.
2. Betsie—more at peace with herself, the homemaker, able to find beauty anywhere. Corrie—more of a rebel, found love for their enemies more difficult.
3. Building of the fake room, obtaining fake ration cards, installing the warning system to be sounded if the Germans came.
4. Hospital worker who gave them vitamins, the lieutenant who let them see their family, the care of the prisoners for each other.
5. Helping persons who had been displaced by the war.

CHALLENGE:

Being able to enjoy the company of the ants, Bible classes in the concentration camp, emotional survival after Betsie's death, strong faith in God and the power of love, learning to forgive those who had persecuted them.

ANSWER KEYS (continued)

Native Son by Richard Wright

OBJECTIVE:

1.	I	6.	G	11.	R	16.	A
2.	B	7.	O	12.	D	17.	L
3.	T	8.	E	13.	J	18.	H
4.	M	9.	S	14.	N	19.	F
5.	Q	10.	K	15.	P	20.	C

SHORT ANSWER:

1. Being shut out from all opportunities and the quality of life that was available to the whites.
2. Bigger meant to keep her from crying out, but he smothered her instead.
3. He was used to being kept "in his place." They treated him like an equal.
4. By a manhunt through the entire city. Finally trapped him on a rooftop.
5. Because Bigger was a horrible animal. Because he was being helped by socialist and communist factions. He represented a danger to the white man's status quo.

CHALLENGE:

The American system dominated by the whites had kept Bigger down. Limits on his life. Slum living conditions. Blacks kept as more an animal or a boy than a man. Loss of hope and opportunity produced the frustration which led to violence.

Index

Anderson, Maxwell	*Elizabeth the Queen*	M	57
Anouilh, Jean	*Becket*	M	59
Borland, Hal	*When the Legends Die*	M	9
Braithwaite, E.R.	*To Sir With Love*	E	105
Brontë, Charlotte	*Jane Eyre*	M	11
Buck, Pearl	*The Good Earth*	M	107
Cormier, Robert	*The Chocolate War*	E	109
Cormier, Robert	*I Am the Cheese*	M	111
Dickens, Charles	*Great Expectations*	M	13
Dickens, Charles	*A Tale of Two Cities*	C	61
Fast, Howard	*April Morning*	E	63
Ferber, Edna	*Cimarron*	M	65
Fitzgerald, F. Scott	*The Great Gatsby*	M	67
Forbes, Esther	*Johnny Tremain*	E	69
Gaines, Ernest J.	*The Autobiography of Miss Jane Pittman*	E	113
Goldman, James	*The Lion in Winter*	M	71
Greene, Bette	*The Summer of My German Soldier*	E	15
Griffin, John Howard	*Black Like Me*	M	115
Hawthorne, Nathaniel	*The House of the Seven Gables*	C	73
Hawthorne, Nathaniel	*The Scarlet Letter*	C	75
Jewett, Sarah Orne	*The Country of the Pointed Firs*	M	77
Hansbury, Lorraine	*A Raisin in the Sun*	M	117
Hellman, Lillian	*The Little Foxes*	M	119
Hinton, S.E.	*Tex*	E	17
Kafka, Franz	*The Metamorphosis*	C	19
Knowles, John	*A Separate Peace*	E	21
Lawrence, Jerome and Robert E. Lee	*Inherit the Wind*	E	121
Lee, Harper	*To Kill a Mockingbird*	M	123
Lee, Robert E. and Jerome Lawrence	*Inherit the Wind*	E	121
Lewis, Sinclair	*Main Street*	M	125
Marshall, Catherine	*Christy*	M	23
McCullers, Carson	*The Heart is a Lonely Hunter*	M	25
McCullers, Carson	*The Member of the Wedding*	M	27
Miller, Arthur	*The Crucible*	M	127
Orwell, George	*Animal Farm*	E	129
Pasternak, Boris	*Doctor Zhivago*	C	79
Paton, Alan	*Cry, the Beloved Country*	M	131
Potok, Chaim	*The Chosen*	M	29
Rose, Reginald	*Twelve Angry Men*	M	133
Salinger, J.D.	*The Catcher in the Rye*	M	31

Schaefer, Jack	Shane	E	33
Seton, Anya	The Winthrop Woman	C	81
Simon, Neil	The Odd Couple	E	35
Spigelgass, Leonard	A Majority of One	M	135
Ten Boom, Corrie	The Hiding Place	E	137
Updike, John	Rabbit, Run	C	37
Uris, Leon	Exodus	C	83
Villasenor, Edmund	Macho	M	39
West, Jessamyn	The Friendly Persuasion	E	85
Wouk, Herman	The Caine Mutiny Court-Martial	M	87
Wright, Richard	Native Son	C	139